DELIGHTING GOD

Delighting God

*How to Live at the
Center of God's Will*

D. James Kennedy, Ph.D.

VINE
BOOKS

Servant Publications
Ann Arbor, Michigan

Vine Books is an imprint of Servant Publications especially
designed to serve Evangelical Christians.

Scripture quotations are from the *King James Version* throughout, unless indicated otherwise.

Published by Servant Publications
P.O. Box 8617
Ann Arbor, Michigan 48107

Cover design by Steve Eames

93 94 95 96 97 10 9 8 7 6 5 4 3 2 1

Printed in the United States of America
ISBN 0-89283-831-0

Library of Congress Cataloging-in-Publication Data

Kennedy, D. James (Dennis James), 1930-
  Delighting God: how to live at the center of God's will/D.
James Kennedy.
     p. cm.
  ISBN 0-89283-831-0
  1. Christian life—Presbyterian authors. I. Title.
BV4501.2.K429 1993
248.4—dc20   93-3610

Contents

How to Really Live

For to be carnally minded is death; but to be spiritually minded is life and peace. Romans 8:6

W hen a little boy returned home from church, his mother asked, "What did the preacher preach about?"

"He didn't say," the boy answered.

In this book I don't intend to make the mistake that preacher made in his sermon. Right here on the first page I'm going to tell you what this book is about. Actually the book's title and subtitle clearly present the theme—Delighting God: How to Live at the Center of God's Will. In other words, this book shows you how to live God's way and places the primary benefit up front: Delighting God.

CHRISTIANITY: CREED AND LIFESTYLE

Right here at the beginning we must ask a basic question: What is Christianity? Some have said that Christianity is not a creed to be believed but a life to be lived. But that doesn't present the full picture. Christianity is both a faith to be believed and a life to be lived.

Yes, it is definitely a creed to be believed. If we believe anything, we have a creed, as the root word, *credo*, means "belief." For example, the pattern throughout the New Testament Epistles—even the whole Bible—presents doctrine and then duty, precept and then practice. *The Shorter Catechism* sums up the teaching of the Scriptures with this question: "What do the Scriptures principally teach?" And the answer: "The Scriptures principally teach what man is to believe concerning God, and what duty God requires of man."

But this does not mean that we are saved by belief plus doing, by faith plus works. No, we are saved by faith alone. But the faith by which we are saved is the faith that inevitably produces good works. Good works is not one of the two horses that pull the carriage of salvation. It is not one of the dual causes of our salvation; good works is, rather, the result of salvation. Good works is not its root but its fruit.

As Christians, what do we believe? The gospel of free grace. This is the message of the Scriptures. It is not merely good advice; it is the good news of the free grace of God. This idea is utterly foreign to the natural human mind. God says that without money or price we may come to him and freely receive that which we in no way deserve. Without character, without morality, without piety, without benevolence, without culture or grooming or education, we can be eternally and everlastingly received into the habitation of God. We can be saved without position or accomplishment, without prayers or study or work or merit, without goodness, or any such thing.

We cannot, however, be saved without Jesus Christ, who becomes our wisdom and righteousness and sanctification and redemption. And when Christ comes into our lives, he produces character and morality and piety.

Actually, that which humanly passes for character or morality or piety in the eyes of God is but filthy rags. Though people think they have all these qualities, if they do not have Christ, they cannot be saved. Scripture says, "Not by works of righteousness which we have done, but according to his mercy he saved us" (Titus 3:5). That is what we are to believe—the free grace of God. We are to repent and put our trust in the Cross of Christ and freely receive the forgiveness of our sins and the gift of everlasting life.

TWO COMMON ERRORS

Someone has said that it is easy to become a prince. It's simply a matter of being born into the right house, of the right parentage. But it is not so easy to live like a prince. If you are a Christian, you are a prince or princess. You have been born into the house of the King of Kings. You are a child of God. How do you live the royal life, delighting the King, honoring the family name?

To answer this question—as we shall throughout this book—we must first warn of two errors. First, let's consider the error of legalism—as it crops up in issues of justification and also sanctification.

Many people believe that if they just do enough good—following the commandments and living by the rules and "doing the best I can," being kind to neighbors, going to church, saying prayers, giving away money—they will gain salvation. This is utterly and completely false to Scripture. Let me repeat what I said above: We are justified by faith without the deeds of the law.

But more subtly legalism often rears its head in the realm of sanctification. Having been made right with God, the believer may turn to a legalistic way of thinking of the Christian life as having an elaborate set of do's and don't's. A believer who becomes enmeshed in these things can lose the very heart of the meaning of Christianity. One of my parishioners put it very aptly in a discussion I had with him. In essence he said:

Here's the trouble with thinking of Christianity as merely a set of rules that mark the boundaries of the path we are to tread: Those who think they have stayed within these boundaries become self-righteous and feel little need for a personal relationship with God to guide them. Because they are living within the boundaries, they believe that all is well. They may even be contemptuous of those they feel are not living within equally confined boundaries. So some people feel self-righteousness and pharisaical pride. Others, who pass beyond their own set boundaries, may feel guilt and despair.

While legalism is an error on one side of a continuum, the opposite error is known as antinomianism, which comes from the Greek word *nomos*, which means *"law."* Antinomian means "against the law." Some people say that once they have been redeemed, once they have come into a personal relationship with Christ, the law has nothing to say to them. At the cross the law was fulfilled, and that was all there was to the law. These people like to say that since they are not under the law but under grace, it doesn't matter whether or not they keep the law. But that is not what the Bible says. Romans 6 says we are not under the law but under grace. What then? Shall we sin because we are not under the law? God forbid! And 1 John 3:4 says that "sin is the transgression of the law."

I remember years ago riding with a friend who drove right through a red light. As he passed under it he said, "Thank heaven, we are not under the law." What chaos if everyone had this attitude. Closing out a passage concerning justification, Paul wrote: "Therefore we conclude that a man is justified by faith without the deeds of the law" (Romans 3:28). Then three verses later he asks, "Do we then make void the law through faith?" Do we do away with the law through faith? Mr. Antinomian would say, "Amen, yes, that's exactly what we do." But Paul continues, giving an answer to his own question: "God forbid: yea, we establish the law."

Referring to the New Covenant under which we now live, God said, "I will... write [the law] in their hearts" (Jeremiah 31:33). Did our Lord Jesus say, "If ye love me, *forget* my commandments"? No, he said, "If ye love me, keep my commandments" (John 14:15).

The antinomian would say that the cross discounted the law

of the sabbath rest. Yet discussing the tribulation that was to come (the earliest event it could have referred to was the destruction of Jerusalem in A.D. 70), Jesus said, "But pray ye that your flight be not in the winter, neither on the sabbath day" (Matthew 24:20). When that flight came, there would still be a sabbath day with which to concern oneself.

In the last book of the Bible, written about A.D. 95, two-thirds of a century after Christ died—after "the law ceased to be," according to the antinomian—we read about the faithful remnant that " ... keep the commandments of God, and have the testimony of Jesus Christ" (Revelation 12:17). Two chapters later John says, "Here is the patience of the saints: here are they that keep the commandments of God, and the faith of Jesus" (Revelation 14:12).

LIVING IN THE CENTER

How do we avoid the evils of antinomianism? How are we going to be lawful without being legalistic? How are we going to be enabled to keep the law of God? How can we keep it without feeling "boxed in" by all these do's and don't's? How can we keep the law of God without becoming self-righteous, thinking we have it made and forgetting about God and our dynamic, personal relationship with him?

Let me suggest three insights from Romans that can help keep a Christian in the center—neither legalistic nor antinomian.

Keeping God's law sets us free. Romans 7 tells us that keeping the law sets us free. It does not enslave us; it does not box us in. Paul says that the law is good; the law is spiritual. It is we who are sinful; it is we who are in bondage by our sinful nature. This is very evident in the case of Adam. God gave him a law—not to eat of the tree of the knowledge of good and evil. That law was given that he might be free. When he broke the law, he ended up in slavery, the abject bondslave of sin. " ... Whosoever committeth sin," said Jesus, "is the servant [*doulos*, bondslave] of sin" (John 8:34).

Compare the law of God with the automobile manual that comes with every new car. It tells you how much air pressure you should have in the tires, how much oil the car needs, how often the oil needs to be changed, and what kind of refrigerant is to be put in the air-conditioning unit.

A person might say, "I just don't like all of these do's and don't's. They are depriving me of my freedom. I'll take that rule book and just throw it away. Nobody's going to tell me I have to go to a filling station all the time and keep putting that oil in there! I've got better things to do." So this person doesn't add oil and eventually the engine just freezes up, stops, way out on a lonely road somewhere. Now this driver is really in a quandry!

You see, the manual wasn't written to enslave; it was written to give an owner all of the freedom that an automobile can provide.

A little sign caught my attention one day: "If all else fails, read the instructions." It's humorous but so true! How many of us want to try to figure it out by ourselves. We're sure we have the answers, even when it comes to life itself. How many of us have had miserable lives because we have not read and heeded the instruction book God has given for this mechanism called the human being? The moral law of God is given by a loving and gracious Father—to allow us to live in liberty. But if we break his law, we are soon going to be living in bondage.

I wonder if anyone could estimate the damage that has been caused in this country because we generally ignore the sabbath rest. Think of the damage to the human body—because we fail to take God's instruction manual seriously; it says we need a period of rest, one day out of seven.

But we're too busy with the rat race—running straight on through the weeks. How many heart attacks, nervous breakdowns, and physical collapses have resulted? How many homes have disintegrated because people have failed to take advantage of the sabbath day to strengthen their spiritual lives so they can better live at peace and harmony with their families? How many souls are on their way to hell because people have ignored the instruction of God's Word? As that sign said, "If all else fails, read the instructions." Follow them and lead a life of freedom.

Christianity is more than keeping the law. Romans 8 tells us that, as we follow the Spirit of God, we fulfill the righteousness of the law. This brings us to the second point: though it is true that keeping the law sets us free, Christianity is more than following a set of rules. It is basically—primarily—a personal relationship.

The Scripture is primarily concerned not with things but with persons. This is the hinge upon which it all turns: personal relationship in doctrine and in duty, in faith and in life. "And this is life eternal, that they might know thee the only true God, and Jesus Christ, whom thou hast sent" (John 17:3). Eternal salvation involves a personal relationship between God and a human being—both here on earth and throughout eternity.

God delights in this relationship—as a husband delights in his relationship with his bride, as a parent delights in his or her relationship with a child. " ... As many as are led by the Spirit of God, they are the sons of God" (Romans 8:14).

The basis for leading the Christian life is a personal relationship with Jesus Christ by his Spirit. Jesus said, "If ye love me, keep my commandments" (John 14:15). You can get different meanings from that sentence, depending on which words you accent. The emphasis should be on "If you *love* me." If that personal relationship of love exists, "keep my commandments." So in knowing him and loving him, we not only receive eternal life, but we also are enabled to follow God and keep the commandments.

Our eyes should be focused on Christ, as the Spirit leads, to follow him, not on the "do" and "don't" signposts at the roadside, which are good guides from our good God. Fix your attention on Christ as the Spirit leads.

I might point out that we are not merely guided; we are *led*. The Greek verb used in Romans 8:14, " ... as many as are led by the Spirit of God, they are the sons of God," is a strong word. It's used other places: referring to an ass and her colt that were *led* to Jesus; referring to Jesus when he was bound and then *led* off to Caiaphas; referring to Jesus who was *led* as a sheep to the slaughter.

The word connotes more than a guidance. It is the living hand of the Spirit guiding and pulling us, drawing us to follow

Jesus Christ as he leads down the center of the path—the center of his will. But also note that it does not imply that we are carried by him. We move under our own locomotion as he enables us and guides us. We are not driven; we are led, and this is the way of Christ.

You know, a certain kind of animal will not follow a shepherd—a goat. The sheep follow but the goats have to be driven. There is a great lesson there. Which are you? When Christ would lead by his precepts, by his example, into what you ought to do and be, do you gladly follow him, or must you be driven with a rod and a whip?

"My sheep hear my voice, and I know them, and they follow me" (John 10:27). In this personal relationship with Christ, we are led by the Holy Spirit down the center of the path, not off into disobedience. We are not boxed in with our eyes on the signpost; they are on Christ the Shepherd, who leads ahead.

As a Christian, you are a child of God. Let's look deeper into the nature of that personal relationship into which we have been ushered. Again I turn to Romans: "Ye have not received the spirit of bondage again to fear; but ye have received the Spirit of adoption, whereby we cry, Abba, Father" (Romans 8:15). As Christians we have been adopted into the family of God. We are no longer slaves, but now we are children. And what God delights in is the willing, joyful obedience of children, not the reluctant, grim, resentful, dour service of the slave. He delights in hearing, "How much can I do?" rather than, "How much must I do?"

Throughout the Old Testament God is repeatedly called Jehovah, but that name doesn't appear once in the Greek New Testament. Why might this be? In the Old Testament God had a different relationship to his people than we do under the New Covenant. We can call God "Abba," an Aramaic word that might be translated as a familiar "Daddy."

At one time my daughter passed through a stage, as many children do, in which she referred to her mother and me as Jim and Anne. I let this go on for a number of days, hoping it was just a passing fancy. But when I saw that she was persisting in this, I thought something should be done.

I took her into the living room and sat her down on my knee and said, "Now, sweetie, I want to tell you something. There are thousands of people in this world who can and do call me Jim, but there is not one single other soul in this world, except you, who can call me Daddy. And to you my name is Daddy. Do you understand?"

The Bible says we have received the spirit of adoption whereby we cry, "Abba, Daddy." Let's say there is an orphanage run by Miss Smith. Mr. Jones comes frequently to see Miss Smith. Little Johnny, who is ten years old, gets to know the visitor and refers to him as Mr. Jones. In time Mr. Jones falls in love with Miss Smith. They marry and move away from the orphanage. But being very fond of little Johnny, they decide to adopt him into their family. Johnny has entered into a new and intimately personal relationship with this man, who is now Daddy.

In the Old Testament God revealed himself as Mr. Jones, as it were. But now we are ushered into a new and intimate relationship through faith in Christ whereby we cry, "Abba, Daddy," with the love of a child to a father who loves with an infinite love.

I know how much I love my only child, Jennifer. It's hard for me to imagine a parent's love being stronger than mine. And yet God's love for me—and you—infinitely surpasses mine—or yours—for a child. Nothing that God would give me, including his law, would be anything but good for me.

DELIGHTING GOD

A number of times throughout the Old Testament we are told what God delights in: "The LORD taketh pleasure in them that fear him, in those that hope in his mercy" (Psalm 147:11). "The steps of a good man are ordered by the LORD: and he [the Lord] delighteth in his way" (Psalm 37:23). "... the prayer of the upright is his [the Lord's] delight" (Proverbs 15:8b).

Here in this book we want to examine what it means to walk

in his will—to delight him, even as he delights in us. But we'll not only examine what this means, we'll discover how we take the steps:

- How do we come into and maintain an intimate relationship with God?
- How do we become mature Christians who "... delight to do thy will, O... God..." (Psalm 40:8)?
- How do we reach beyond ourselves and allow God to use us to transform our relationships and our world?

Each chapter ends with a "For Reflection" section. Here I ask you to examine your life and your relationship with God. In what specific area is his voice speaking to you? What adjustments is he asking you to take as he directs your steps into the center of his will?

My prayer is that God will use the words in these pages to bring you and your world into a relationship of delight with him.

D. James Kennedy, Ph.D.

Part One

You and Your Relationship with God

ONE

How to Be Right with God

Therefore we conclude that a man is justified by faith without the deeds of the law. **Romans 3:28**

JUSTIFICATION. It is a musty, dusty word, reminiscent of law books and tomes of legal evidence. There is something uninteresting about the whole subject, unless, of course, you happen to be the center of focus in a courtroom, where all eyes are turned on you—accused of a heinous crime.

At one point that was the case with Feodor Dostoevski, one of the greatest novelists of all time. During the reign of the czars, he got himself involved with a group of would-be revolutionaries. One day the police swept down and hauled them off to jail, into court—where they were condemned and sentenced: death by a firing squad!

And so on one winter morning in Russia, when the temperature had plummeted below zero, they were stripped, given a shroud to wear, and marched single file out into the courtyard, past a stack of coffins painted black. They were lined up before a wall and a funeral service was read to them.

Being number four in line, Dostoevski estimated that he had approximately four minutes of life remaining. He quickly determined to savor those minutes as a man in the Sahara might savor the last ounce of water in his canteen. He meticulously divided up the minutes. For one minute he would think of all the pleasant experiences he had had in his life. For the next minute he would remember all of his loved ones. For the third minute he would look about him—at the sky and clouds and the trees—and savor the beauty of this creation, which soon would disappear into a black chasm before his eyes. In the fourth minute he would lift his eyes to God.

Suddenly, he heard a horse's gallop. A man on horseback appeared across the courtyard and handed the commanding lieutenant a pardon from the czar. As it turned out, the whole incident was a sham intended to intimidate.

This encounter—standing on the precipice of eternity—marked these men for the rest of their lives. Several of them lost their minds completely. As for Dostoevski, the matter of judgment and pardon, of justice and justification, spilled from his pen onto the pages of his books. It is not possible to read his writings without sensing his acute awareness of life-and-death issues.

Actually, his dramatic situation is not all that unique. One day each of us will stand in front of the judgment seat of God. Will we be declared guiltless or guilty? For answers let's look at a portion of Romans 3.

In his commentary of Romans, Martin Luther wrote this marginal note regarding Romans 3:28: "Note well what is here said, for this is the central, the most important paragraph in the most important episode—no—indeed, the most important paragraph in all of Scripture." John Calvin concurred, saying that no other passage in all of Scripture has such significance concerning God's method of justifying humanity by righteousness.

What does this "most important paragraph" say? "Therefore we conclude that a man is justified by faith without the deeds of the law." This is indeed the central citadel of Scripture. It is the very heart of the body of revealed truth; it is the most important message the world has ever heard. And yet millions still perish in ignorance of this great truth.

ALL HAVE SINNED

Romans 3:28 is the culmination of a longer passage. Beginning with verse 10, Paul catalogs the sin of humanity: "As it is written, There is none righteous, no, not one: There is none that understandeth, there is none that seeketh after God. They are all gone out of the way, they are together become unprofitable; there is none that doeth good, no, not one" (vv. 10-12). Paul lays the whole world under the condemnation of sin. This is evident also in the Old Testament: "For there is not a just man upon earth, that doeth good, and sinneth not" (Ecclesiastes 7:20).

I recall speaking to a man who said he didn't believe in sin or that people were sinful. He believed that people were good.

"Is that a fact?" I said.

He replied, "Yes, that is a fact."

I asked, "May I see your keys?"

He reached in his pocket and pulled out his key chain. I responded, "If you don't believe that people are sinful, why do you have these keys?"

He just stared at me with a blank look.

The front page of the daily paper attests to the fact that all have sinned and come short of the glory of God, just as Paul clearly says in Romans 3:23. There he lays low the pride of humanity, smites us in the forehead, and exposes our sin.

The first great point contained in this Romans 3 passage is that there is none righteous. In thought, in word, in deed, in omission and in commission, all have fallen short of the glory of God.

WE CANNOT HELP OURSELVES

But Paul doesn't end there. In verse 19, he says: "Now we know that what things soever the law saith, it saith to them who are under the law: that every mouth may be stopped, and all the world may become guilty before God." He's saying that there is nothing we can do to make ourselves acceptable to God.

That is the very verse the Holy Spirit used to bring *this sin-*

ner into a relationship with Christ. More than thirty-eight years ago my morning slumbers were broken by an alarm-clock radio. Over the airwaves I heard a preacher, Dr. Donald Grey Barnhouse, expounding on this text, and that proclamation utterly, totally, eternally changed my life.

Some years later, Dr. Barnhouse's widow sent me a copy of his book, *Your Right to Heaven* (Baker Book House, 1977) based on his sermons. Her inscription acknowledged her husband's influence on my ministry. Inside, on the appropriate page, she had written a note in the margin: "These are the words you heard over your radio that morning."

I would like to pay tribute to Dr. Barnhouse, a great preacher of the gospel, by repeating several illustrations he gave in that message. The Holy Spirit used them to speak to my heart; I trust they will touch yours.

The law does not justify. Dr. Barnhouse told of being invited to address a combined meeting of a city's Kiwanis Club, Lions Club, and Rotary Club. After Dr. Barnhouse had clearly set forth God's method of justifying sinners, many Christians in the group came up, heartily shook his hand, and thanked him for the wonderful exposition of the gospel.

One of the Christians quietly commented on another man in the room. "Do you see that portly man approaching? He is a millionaire, and he has a trick question that he asks every guest preacher. He's coming now to ask you, and the question is…"

At that point in the sentence, the man arrived and introduced himself. Dr. Barnhouse prepared himself for the onslaught, though he still felt somewhat in the dark, not knowing the question.

Sure enough, the man said he had a question he wanted to ask. But he wanted assurance that he would be given a yes-or-no answer.

Dr. Barnhouse quickly replied, "Some questions just cannot be answered with a yes or no. Suppose I ask you this: Have you stopped beating your wife? Yes or no?"

Silence!

Dr. Barnhouse continued by assuring the man that he would do his best to be succinct.

Here was the question: "I am a Jew, and all my life I have tried to keep the commandments and live by the precepts of God given in the Old Testament. Tell me: Do you believe that I will be accepted into heaven?"

Dr. Barnhouse gave a brilliant answer. "Tell me, who do you think was the greatest man in all the Old Testament?"

"Why, Moses, of course."

"Without any hesitation, I can tell you that you will be received into heaven in precisely the same way that Moses was received."

At this point the man's face was wreathed in smiles. He said, "Thank you, Doctor. I am delighted to see that you are a broad-minded man."

Dr. Barnhouse kept talking, "But tell me, sir. How was Moses accepted into heaven?"

The man replied, "Why, by keeping the law, of course."

Dr. Barnhouse held out his Bible and said, "Sir, I will give a thousand dollars to a charity of your choice if you can show me as much as one verse in all of this book that says that Moses got to heaven by keeping the law."

The man looked at the book, then at Dr. Barnhouse. He didn't reach out a hand. With somewhat less assurance he said, "Well, then how did Moses get to heaven?"

Dr. Barnhouse replied, "Moses got to heaven—he was accepted by God—when Aaron, his brother the high priest, brought a lamb; Moses confessed his sins over that lamb; the lamb was slain; the lamb's blood was shed."

The Old Testament clearly states that without the shedding of blood there is no remission of sin. We are not saved by what we do. Again, the Bible makes it clear that no one has ever kept the precepts or commandments of the Old Testament, much less the New Testament, which says those commands refer to thoughts—of hatred and lust, for instance—as well as deeds.

The law shows us our sinfulness. Many people are surprised when they fully understand God's method of justifying sinners. Romans 3:19 states: "Now we know that what things soever the law saith, it saith to them who are under the law: that every mouth may be stopped, and all the world may become..." Become what? "Become guilty before God." Most people suppose that the law was given that people might become righteous. But the purpose of the law is to show us what we are doing wrong.

Martin Luther said that the law was a mirror that showed us our uncleanness. The law was a hammer that smashed our self-righteousness. The law was a whip that drove us to the cross to find mercy, for no mere human being has ever kept the law of God.

Dr. Barnhouse told another story of a conversation he had with a man who said that he didn't need the church or Christianity because he was a member of a particular lodge. He believed that he would gain admission to heaven by keeping the organization's obligations.

Some years later Dr. Barnhouse heard that this man was seriously ill. He went to see him in the hospital. He went into the room, sat down in the chair next to the bed but didn't say a word even though he knew the man was expected to die within hours. This being an extreme case, he thought extreme measures were necessary. He continued to sit there, looking at the man in the bed.

The man returned the look quizzically, until Dr. Barnhouse said, "You've always said that you didn't need Christ; you didn't need the church; you would get to heaven by keeping the obligations of your lodge. I have always wanted to see how such a man died. You don't mind if I just sit here and watch, do you?"

The man, according to Dr. Barnhouse, had a look on his face like a wounded animal. He stammered, "You wouldn't mock a dying man, would you?"

Dr. Barnhouse pressed him, asking what his hopes were at this point in his life. Was the lodge enough? The man knew he was about to leap into the blackness of an uncertain eternity. Dr. Barnhouse again shared the glorious gospel of grace. At the last hours of this man's life, he entered into the mercy and forgiveness and grace of God, for he had discovered this great truth: "... by the deeds of the law there shall no flesh be justified in his sight: for by the law is the knowledge of sin" (Romans 3:20).

I, like the dying man, had built a great toothpick-citadel of theology—a great castle of my views of a person's relationship to God. And with the preaching of this Romans passage, that whole citadel crumbled to the ground. Note well: The law was given to show you that you are a sinner, not to provide any hope for your acceptance into the kingdom of God.

Dr. Barnhouse told of yet another conversation he had with a young marine lieutenant. When asked what he would say to God when standing at the final judgment, the marine responded, "I would simply stand by my record."

Dr. Barnhouse continued with a fictional story about a man who drove the wrong way up a one-way street. Going fifty miles an hour, he ran through several red lights, hit a parked car but kept going, tried to evade the police. When he was finally pulled over to the curb, he slapped the policeman and resisted arrest.

Restrained by handcuffs and dragged into court, the man faced the judge, who asked, "How do you plead?"

The man said, "Judge, I'll just stand on my record."

The judge had the last word. "Young man, it is your record that has brought you here, and it is your record that is going to put you in jail."

And so it is with us. Our record is our condemnation—not our salvation. "By the deeds of the law there shall no flesh be justified in his sight."

GOD'S GRACE

After showing the plight of humanity and our inability to do anything to justify ourselves, we come now to the third great point in Romans 3. Paul reveals God's method for justifying sinners. After having dug a ditch, a hole, a pit so deep that the light above was obscured, Paul finally introduced God's revelation of the solution to the mystery of our acceptance into his kingdom: "But now the righteousness of God without the law is manifested" (Romans 3:21a).

The righteousness of God. There came a time in his life when Martin Luther had a new understanding of this phrase. He had previously hated the concept. Whenever the righteousness of God had come to mind, he had thought of God's character, his holiness, justice, purity, his wrath against sin, and he had felt condemned and overwhelmed.

But finally he discovered new meaning in the righteousness of God: By faith in Jesus Christ the righteousness of God was imputed unto all and upon all who believe. Here in Romans Paul was not referring to the character of God in heaven but to the earned and merited righteousness of the God-man, Jesus Christ; by thirty-three years of perfect obedience to God, he obtained a white robe of perfect righteousness, which can become ours by faith in him.

When you and I stand before the Almighty there are two things we must have—two things without which we have no hope of acceptance. Note well what they are: First, you must have a record of *100 percent perfect obedience* to every commandment of God— in thought, in word, in deed, in omission, and in commission. If you offend in one point, you are guilty of all. Heaven is a perfect place into which only perfect people will be admitted. Second, you must have a record of *no sin whatsoever!* Unless you have no sin and perfect obedience, I assure you, on the basis of God's Word, that you will never enter that city of gold.

Do you have such a perfect record? I want to tell you that I do. I have a robe of perfect whiteness, perfect obedience. But let me hasten to add that it is not inherently my own. I didn't live it, and I didn't earn it. It was lived and earned by Jesus Christ; by his shed blood upon the cross. He has washed me from every stain of sin. By his sinlessness and perfect obedience of thirty-three years, he has earned a white robe of righteousness.

And I stand clothed in that righteousness of his, faultless, able to stand before the throne of God.

Are you clothed in those lustrous garments? Do you have what is required to enter heaven? Paul says, "Being justified freely by his grace through the redemption that is in Christ Jesus" (Romans 3:24). To be justified by his grace means to be justified without any reason in ourselves, holy without any merit of our own.

Many people have little understanding of these matters. They hope that they deserve a reward. But salvation is not based on human desert in the least. We are justified not because of what we have done; we are justified *in spite* of everything we have done! We are justified because of what God has done for us in Christ. We are justified by his grace through the redemption that is in Christ Jesus.

JUSTIFICATION THROUGH FAITH IN CHRIST

The fourth point we see in Romans 3 is that God is able to justify sinners through the redemption that is in Christ Jesus. Throughout his whole life Socrates wrestled with a question for which he never discovered an answer. He thought it might be possible that a just and holy God could pardon guilty and sinful sinners and yet still remain just—but he didn't really see how it could be.

On the wall of the Supreme Court in Washington, D.C., is this motto: "When the guilty is acquitted, the judge is condemned." If a person guilty of capital crimes were brought before a judge and let go or just slapped on the wrist, the newspaper would be filled with the indignation of writers railing against injustice.

How can a holy and just God forgive sinful and guilty sinners and still remain just? After all, the essence of justice is that virtue (of which we have none) be rewarded and vice (of which we have much) be punished. The answer is found in the redemption that is in Christ Jesus, "Whom God hath set forth to be a propitiation through faith in his blood" (Romans 3:25a).

What is *propitiation*? That which makes propitious or well-pleasing. God is angry with the wicked—pouring out wrath upon sinners. We stand beneath that wrath. But Christ came to push us aside; he took his place on the cross, and there the wrath of God fell upon him—in our place; the justice of God was fulfilled. And we are spared—if we believe in and accept the substitutionary nature of his atoning death.

That is why Paul goes on to say, "To declare, I say, at this time, his [Jesus'] righteousness: that he [Jesus] might be just, and the justifier of him which believeth in Jesus" (Romans 3:26).

Did you hear that, Socrates? "That he [Jesus] might be just" and forgive sinners as "the justifier" of those who believe in him, the propitiation. There on the cross our sin was imputed to the sinless Christ. Justice is fulfilled because his blood was shed to cover the punishment of our sin. Mercy is revealed; the sinner is spared. This is the glorious wonder of the gospel of Jesus' grace: totally unmerited and undeserved favor.

Paul continues. "Where is boasting then? It is excluded. By what law? of works? Nay: but by the law of faith [of grace]" (Romans 3:27).

I know beyond any doubt that if I were to drop dead this very moment, I will be in paradise forever with God. But there is no boasting in that statement. Why? Though I know I am going to heaven, I know equally well that I deserve to go to hell. The only reason I will go to heaven is because Christ went to hell for me on the cross. "He that glorieth [boasteth], let him glory in the Lord" (1 Corinthians 1:31b). Christ is our boast. Christ is our glory. He is the boast of every true believer.

As a great hymn says, "In the Cross of Christ I glory"—the cross that towers over us humans, "the wrecks of time."

CHRIST ALONE IS THE ANSWER

Here at last we come to the pinnacle of the final paragraph—the great summation of the gospel of Jesus Christ. "Therefore we conclude that a man is justified by faith without the deeds of the law" (Romans 3:28). It is by faith in the Cross of Jesus Christ alone that we are justified.

But may I propose that some people get so close to the kingdom of God and yet they remain so far away. They suppose they have faith in Christ, but they are trusting merely in the teachings of Christ. The teachings of Christ will not save you. The preaching of Christ will not save you. The example of Christ will not save you. He was the greatest teacher, the greatest preacher, and the greatest exemplar who ever lived. But all of those attributes combined do only one thing: They condemn you because you have not lived by the teaching of Christ; you have not lived by the preaching of Christ. Next to Jesus Christ, all of your warts and wrinkles and vileness and sin stand out in stark contrast.

No, it is the blood of Jesus Christ that saves. Remember what Paul says: "Being justified freely by his grace.... Whom God hath set forth to be a propitiation through faith in his blood... (Romans 3:24, 25). Without the shedding of blood there is no remission of sins. That is the bull's-eye of the entire gospel. We must trust in the Cross of Christ—not the teachings of Christ, not the ethics of Christ, not the philosophy of Christ, not the example of Christ.

We conclude that anyone who trusts in that cross is justified, apart from good works, apart from keeping the law; aside from anything whatsoever that you or I have done, Jesus paid the full price of our salvation. The great preacher Charles Spurgeon said that if we had to put one stitch into the garment of our salvation, we would ruin the whole thing. It is by faith in Christ alone that we are saved.

You may ask, "Why should I then try to live a good life?" There are two basic motives. The first is futile: to gain or earn eternal life. The second is noble: to show my gratitude for an eternal life that I have been given by his grace, through Jesus Christ.

The first and last verses of another old hymn, by Isaac Watts, poetically summarize a Christian's relationship to the Christ of the cross:

When I survey the wondrous cross,
On which the Prince of glory died,
My richest gain I count my loss,
And pour contempt on all my pride.

Were the whole realm of nature mine,
That were a present far too small;
Love so amazing, so divine,
Demands my soul, my life, my all.

FOR REFLECTION

Have you been justified by Christ's righteousness imputed to you? Are you ready to stand before God? Do you know assuredly that it shall be well with your soul on that great judgment day?

If not, I urge you to abandon all trust in yourself—the obligations of your church, the commandments of the Scripture, your own morality or piety—and to flee to the cross. Humbly kneeling in the presence of God, appeal to Christ to cleanse you by his blood and clothe you in the robe of his righteousness.

Then stand and rejoice—knowing that you will stand faultless before his throne someday. Through Christ you have been made right with God. You now have a wonderful opportunity to get to know him.

TWO

How to Know God

And this is life eternal, that they might know thee the only true God, and Jesus Christ, whom thou hast sent. John 17:3

I N THE STRICTEST and truest sense of the word, Christianity is not a religion; it is a relationship. The Latin root of the noun *religion* is *religare*, which has two meanings, "to bind" and "to hold back"—two common aspects of all pagan religions.

What do I mean? First, they attempt, usually by sacrifices, to bind God to humankind. Second, they try to hold back or restrain human conduct by a system of laws or proscriptions. But not one of these pagan religions has a gospel—a "good news" message of justification. There are many rules and many sets of ethics and commandments, but there is no gospel to be found anywhere, except in Christianity. Pagan religions are based upon a "do this" and "don't do that" attempt to bind God to humanity and by proscriptions and commandments to hold back the more vicious aspects of human nature.

CHRISTIANITY IS A RELATIONSHIP

But Christianity is quite different. It is a relationship between Christ and a human soul. It is the most intimate and personal

31

kind of relationship—an intimate communion with our dearest friend. That was what Christ was talking about when he prayed to the Father: "that he [Jesus, the Son] should give eternal life to as many as thou hast given him. And this is life eternal, that they might know thee the only true God, and Jesus Christ, whom thou hast sent" (John 17:2-3). God has a people whom he has chosen. He has given this people to Christ, and Christ is to give to each of them eternal life, which he describes in terms of a relationship.

In this passage the Greek word *hautay*, meaning "this," is placed in the position of emphasis. Christ is saying that he is going to give them eternal life. "And *this* is life eternal, that they might know thee, the only true God."

Eternal life is not piling ages upon ages in heaven. It begins right now. It begins with a whole new dimension, a different quality of life alien and foreign to the life of this world. It is the very life of God. To have eternal life, to be a Christian, to discover salvation—all these realities come together when we know God, "the only true God, and Jesus Christ, whom thou hast sent."

WHAT DOES IT MEAN TO KNOW GOD?

In the Bible (Hebrew and Greek) and even today, the word *know* has two very different connotations. Sometimes we use the word to refer to someone's intellectual understanding: someone knows their facts or figures.

Many people think they know God in this fashion—intellectually. Some—atheists—"know" that God doesn't exist. Some—agnostics—don't deny God's existence but say, *"I just don't know."* Repeatedly the apostle Paul said, "… I would not have you to be agnostic, brethren,…" (1 Thessalonians 4:13), except that in the English translation it is, "I would not have you to be ignorant, brethren." The word *ignorant* is an exact equivalent of "agnostic" (one taken from the Greek and the other taken from the Latin). So the next time you meet someone who claims to be an agnostic, you might express sympathy that he or she is so ignorant! The Bible says that God would not have us be ignorant.

If we were categorizing people and their knowledge of God in steps, above the atheist and the agnostic we might come to the theist who believes that a god exists but doesn't know who God is or what he is like or how he may be known.

Above that, we come to the professing Christians (about 85 percent of the American people profess themselves to be Christians) who do not possess what they profess. They may know a lot *about* him. They may intellectually understand his omniscience, his omnipresence, his omnipotence, but this knowledge is still of the intellect. It might be appropriate, in many of their churches, to bring that idol from Athens that Paul referred to when he said in effect, "I saw your idols... that you are altogether too superstitious. You have even an idol to the unknown god" (see Acts 17:22-23). There are millions this day worshiping, or at least pretending to worship, a god they think they know about, but he is really unknown to them.

But in the Bible—and still today in English—the word *know* also refers to the most intimate of personal experiences—where two people become one. We read in the Old Testament that Adam "knew" Eve, and she conceived and brought forth a child.

This is eternal life as described by Jesus—to *know* God in the most intimate personal way. Theologians call it a mystical union between Christ and the human soul. Of course this is not a physically sexual union, but a mystical heart-to-heart and soul-to-soul intimacy. Christ is our Bridegroom, and we are the bride. This relationship is what Christianity is. This is what salvation is. This is what eternal life is.

We can describe the Christian doctrine of salvation in a number of different metaphors. In chapter one we used terms from the courtroom, particularly justification—where a judge declares someone not guilty.

We can also describe salvation biologically, as in the "new birth" that Jesus declared: "Except a man be born again, he cannot see the kingdom of God" (John 3:3b).

But the essence of salvation is not simply to pardon us. It is not even that we might be born into his family as his children, but that, having been born into his family, we might come to know him and have an intimate, personal relationship with him. That is the purpose of eternal life—that we might know God intimately, experientially, in the laboratory of our own hearts and souls, as Jesus Christ, who is God, comes and lives in our hearts.

On the last night before Jesus was crucified—the same night that he prayed this prayer recorded in John 17—he was trying to instruct his disciples. Philip—expressing the hunger of the whole human race—said: "... Lord, shew us the Father, and it sufficeth us" (John 14:8). He didn't want much—just bring God down that we might see him and "that is enough."

How did Jesus answer? He said, "... [Philip] he that hath seen me, hath seen the Father...." (John 14:9).

I remember visiting in a home, discussing spiritual things with a gentleman. I said, "The Scriptures teach that Jesus Christ, Jesus of Nazareth, was, and is eternally, the everlasting, all-powerful, all-wise God." The word *God* had not ceased its reverberations in the room, before his eyes filled with tears. This man in his fifties, who had been in the church all of his life, said, "I never heard that before, but I always thought that's how it ought to be."

How right he was. That is how it is. People say, "God ought to be like Jesus." Yes, God is like Jesus because Jesus is God, the Second Person of the Triune Godhead: Father, Son, and the Holy Spirit. He is the Creator of the universe, the Redeemer of humankind, the one who will be the Judge of all humanity. Jesus is God. To know him is to know God. We could never intimately, personally know God apart from Christ.

We would be like blind people groping in the darkness if God had not condescended to reveal himself, if he had not come so that the human eye could see him, the human ear could hear him, the human hand could touch him. To know him personally—not just know about him—is the greatest thing in the world. This is eternal life.

Pascal, the renowned French philosopher and scientist, said that there is a "God-shaped vacuum" in the human heart that cannot be filled by anything but God. Augustine said, "Our hearts are restless till they rest in Thee."

Even the atheist existential philosopher Jean Paul Sartre said, "Everything in myself calls for God, and that I can't forget." That is the hungering of the human heart. Men and women try to fill it with every sort of thing—with this toy and that gadget, with this experience and that diversion. They go from one thing to another, not knowing that you can't fly a jet plane on tomato juice, and you can't fill a human heart with gadgets. Only Christ can fill it.

The psalmist described it beautifully—talking not about the heart within, but about the hart in the forest, the stag, the deer. He said, "As the hart panteth after the water brooks, so panteth my soul after thee, O God" (Psalm 42:1).

Some of you have been longing, panting, hungering, thirsting, but you didn't even know what you were thirsting for! It is only God who can end that longing, that restlessness, that emptiness, that lovelessness. Only the great Lover of our souls can fill that need. Do you know him? Have you experienced that knowledge of Christ?

C.S. Lewis once referred to a conversation he was having with a man who casually mentioned, "I have known God." It struck Lewis that a person so simply and plainly would make a statement so profound. "I have known God." I wonder how many of you could say that?

HOW CAN WE KNOW GOD?

How can we know God? We can come to know God through Jesus Christ. God has come into this world in the person of his Son so that we might know him. If we receive Christ into our hearts by faith, if we place our trust in his atoning death, if we cease to trust in all of our goodness and good works and religiosity and morality, if we place our whole hope in him who died as our substitute upon that cruel tree, we will enter into a personal relationship with God.

As we grow in the Christian life we come to know Christ better. In fact, we are admonished in the New Testament to "... grow in grace, and in the knowledge of our Lord and Savior Jesus Christ...." (2 Peter 3:18). "Maturing in the Christian life," "growing in grace," "advancing in sanctification"—these are simply different ways of stating that we are coming to know Christ better—just as any earthly relationship grows with time and tender care. When someone first comes into our lives, we know them personally, but the intimacy of the relationship grows closer and more as we come to know that person better.

An old popular song starts, "Getting to know you, getting to know all about you...." How do we get to know God better? In time and in these three ways as suggested in the Bible:

By stillness. "Be still, and know that I am God" (Psalm 46:10). If there is one thing that people today cannot abide, it is stillness! We are constantly bombarded by noise, from the television, radio, stereo, or even a Walkman or a boombox! Most of us can't stand much silent time.

How few people today have a significant quiet time where they get alone with God. How few spend time reading his Word, which is full of accounts of his dealings with us. But more than that, how few spend quiet time praying to him, talking to him and listening to his voice, getting to know him. This is what Jesus was talking about when he said, "... enter into thy closet [your inner chamber], and when thou hast shut thy door, pray to thy Father which is in secret..." (Matthew 6:6). He was talking about having a quiet place for a quiet time.

If we are going to get to know our children, we have to spend time with them. The myth about "quality" time has often been an excuse for being too busy with too many other things to spend time with loved ones. We wonder why children drift away and why couples break apart. How many are so busy with so many other things, they haven't set aside time just to be with one another, to be at one, to get to know one another, and to appreciate one another? We need to spend that quiet time with God; we need to be still and know down in the depths of our souls that he is God.

By obedience. Second, the Bible says that we can know him by *obedience*. The Scripture tells us that we will get to know him better as we do the things he has told us. "And Moses said, Hereby ye shall know that the LORD hath sent me to do all these works; for *I have* not *done them* of mine own mind" (Numbers 16:28). Those who do the will of God will know whether all of this comes from God, whether this is, indeed, God's Book, God's Word, God's will, God's salvation—by obedience.

There are some who will say, "Well, that doesn't make sense. We don't obey in order to know; we know in order to obey." That is true in many cases but not always. Consider Thomas Edison. In trying to make an incandescent light bulb, he tried hundreds of different filaments; one after another after another, none would work. Finally, he tried a new element and it did work. Light! He then knew what worked because he had finally obeyed the laws that God had put into this world. By doing he had come to know. So we know and therefore we do; we do and therefore we know more.

It is impossible to grow in a relationship with Christ while living in disobedience to him. We must repent of our sins and say, "O Christ, it is my great desire to live for you; to be the person you want me to be; to do those things you would have me to do. Lord, I want to know you better and better."

Are you living the life of obedience to Christ? In what areas are you habitually disobeying Christ? Some of you don't tithe and bring your offerings, and you wonder why God seems far away. Some of you are disobeying God in that you don't witness for Christ. This week has passed, and you have told no one the gospel. This month has passed, and you have told no one the gospel. This year has passed, you've told no one the gospel. And yet the first and last commands of Christ were to go and share the gospel. You have been living in disobedience to him. If you would know him, you must obey him.

By loving God. Third, we come to know God better by loving him. Someone might say, "Well, we can love someone only if we know that person." On a human level of relationship that is often the case. But what is usually true in this world is often the reverse in the spiritual world. In fact, the Bible says "... every one that loveth is born of God, and knoweth God... for God is love" (1 John 4:7-8). We need to express our love to him; we need to love him as we ought to love and to love all about us as he taught us to love.

A LESSON FROM JESUS' ENCOUNTER WITH PHILIP

An interesting story in the first chapter of John describes why so many people don't know God as intimately as they might. John the Baptist had been baptizing. He was standing at the brink of the Jordan River along with two of his disciples. Jesus came walking past them, and John uttered those great words of identification: "... Behold the Lamb of God, which taketh away the sin of the world" (John 1:29). And the two disciples followed Jesus. Jesus, perceiving that they followed him, turned and said to them, "What seek ye?"

They replied, "Where dwelleth thou?"

Jesus said, "Come and see" (vv. 38-39).

I seriously doubt that it was to any house, because the Son of Man had no where to lay his head, but wherever it was, they "abode with him that day" (v. 39). Later, Philip, one of the two, went and found his brother Peter and brought him to Jesus. Did you see all of the dynamics that took place there?

Jesus said, "Come." And later Philip went and found his brother Peter, sharing the good news he'd discovered. But

between the "come" and the "go" (witness) there was "abide"
—something that is often missing in the lives of Christians today.
Philip spent time with him, getting to know him, learning about
him, sharing his heart and his thoughts.

The apostle John recorded this account of Philip meeting
Jesus, the same Gospel writer who recorded Jesus' prayer the
night of his crucifixion: "And this is life eternal, that they might
know thee the only true God, and Jesus Christ, whom thou
hast sent" (John 17:3).

That life eternal begins here and now. The greatest thing in
this world or in the world to come, that which is life itself, is to
come to know God.

And when it comes to knowing God, the old love song holds
true: "To know you is to love you." In the next chapter we'll
look more closely at what it means to love God.

FOR REFLECTION

Do you know God? Do you know him as you would like to
know him? If your soul pants for a more intimate relationship
with the living God, spend time today, this week, abiding with
him in a quiet place. Read his Word, obey his Word, listen to
his voice communing with your spirit. Spend time with him,
and you will come to know him who loves you with a love that
is beyond human love. You will find the fulfillment of your
heart's desire.

THREE

How to Love God

Thou shalt love the Lord thy God with all thy heart, and with all thy soul, and with all thy mind. This is the first and great commandment. Matthew 22:37-38

A MOTHER, HELPING her ten-year-old daughter with bedtime prayers suggested, "Darling, why don't you pray that the Lord would help you to love him more?"

The little girl looked up with some surprise. "You want me to pray that God would help me to love him more?"

"Yes."

The girl answered, "All right, Mom, but I'm just crazy about him already!"

How many of us feel the same way? What did Jesus call the "first and great commandment"? "Thou shalt love the Lord thy God with all thy heart and with all thy soul, and with all thy mind." It really does not make much difference if we say we have kept other commandments—we have not stolen, we have not killed—if we have broken the first and greatest commandment and have not loved God with all of our hearts.

How many times have I heard people say, "Oh, well I think I would be acceptable to God; after all, I have never hurt anyone." These people are completely oblivious to the fact that they have not loved God with all of their hearts and are there-fore guilty of having broken the greatest commandment of all!

Many people in the church might be ever so punctilious in a thousand little things; they might mortify themselves in numer-ous ways until life becomes joyless and passionless. They wear themselves out serving on committees and in various efforts until they almost drop with fatigue. Yet God is not pleased in the least with anything they have done because it has not sprung from a heart that loves him. Do you really love God? The commandment is obviously important if we are to have a relationship with God that delights him.

THE GREAT COMMANDMENT

Can you imagine someone commanding love? We could easily understand how God could command us to do what he wants us to do. After all, he is our Creator! We could even understand how he could command us to say what we should say or even to think what he would have us think. And he does, indeed, do that. He says that every thought should be brought into captivity to Jesus Christ (see 2 Corinthians 10:5). But to go into that inner-most closet, that deepest recess of the human heart where we guard our love and affection and to say that we must love, to command us to love, seems to be a contradiction of love. At least this one secret place should be private. And yet God commands us to love!

Can you imagine saying to anyone, "Thou shalt love me!" God does not command some vague or general or even partial kind of love. But he says that we are to love him! We *shall* love him with all of our heart and mind and strength and soul; it shall be an all-encompassing, intensive love for God. Furthermore, we are told that not having this love is the greatest and worst sin that we are capable of committing. Did you ever think about that?

Why is this the case? I see several reasons. God knows that we are going to love something supremely. If we do not love him, we are going to love something less noble, something less honorable, something less glorious, something less exalted than God. And when we do that, we are inevitably going to become like the object we love in the same way that we become like that which we worship. That is why God says that he is a jealous God, that we should have no other gods before him.

It is important that we worship the one true God. Why? Because God knows that if we do not, we will suffer. It is not that God needs our love; it is not that God needs our worship. God does not need anything! He is perfect. But *we* need him. We need to worship him and we need to love him and delight in him so that our lives might be purified by that love. In centuries gone by there was a common saying in England: Nothing under heaven was more effective in shaping a man than the love of a good woman. These days we may not hear sentiments like that expressed, but I think there is still a lot of truth in it. And as Christians our lives are shaped as we grow in our love relationship with God.

God has also ordered us to love him because he knows that our biggest problem is selfishness. In fact, the root and essence of sin is selfishness, which is the very antithesis of love. When we love another we are going against all the basic selfish instincts of our fallen human nature. If we are going to be lifted out of the mire of our sin and depravity, it is going to be by the power of love.

BUT PEOPLE DO NOT LOVE GOD

It is tragic that so many people very obviously do not love God. There are people who blaspheme his name, who deny him, who become vehement at the mention of him. It is amazing to me that atheists can become so hostile to something they claim does not exist.

Many other people are indifferent; they think very little about God. Maybe the only time they use God's name is in profanity. But let me make it very clear: You cannot use God's name in vain and love him! Any person who takes the name of God in vain is holding up a sign saying that he or she does not love God! If you love your mother, you will not drag her name in the mud, and if you love God, you will not drag his name in the mud. I can say to the glory of God that from the very moment I accepted Jesus Christ as my Savior, I ceased taking his name in vain. And that happens to every true believer, because we begin to love him.

Many other people are lukewarm in their relationship with God. They go about day after day with little or no thought of God. God—consuming their thoughts and their passions? You might as well be talking about Mars consuming their passions. They certainly do not obey the first and greatest command-ment—to love God, especially, as Jesus said, "with all of thine heart."

LOVE FOR GOD STARTS IN THE HEART

Love God—"with all of thy heart, and with all of thy soul, and with all thy mind." Mark and Luke both add, "with all of thy strength." You will notice that Jesus begins with the heart. It has often been said that words without actions mean nothing. How many people speak eloquent words, religious words, and yet their actions do not back them up? We sometimes fail to remember that eloquent words and tireless actions on behalf of the cause of Christ may mean nothing at all.

The Pharisees were eloquent and fastidious in their various activities for God, and yet because there was no love in their hearts for him, because these actions stemmed from a sterile legalism or concern about what other people would say about them, the motive, the spring that caused these things to come forth, was not the love of God. Jesus says that they were totally unacceptable to him. I am afraid that many people in the church are engaged in many activities for the wrong reasons.

The Scriptures make it very plain: No work is good that is not done for the right motive.

What is your motive for serving Christ with all of your heart and with all of your soul? There are people whose affections, it seems, can be touched very easily. Their emotional cup is full and they brim over. They can be touched by any sort of thing— a poem, a sunset, a picture—and yet their spiritual sense might be dull and stunted. They are not really touched and gripped by the holiness of God. They can come to a communion service and go away and very shortly become involved in things that are unholy and unclean.

LOVING GOD WITH YOUR SOUL AND MIND

To love God with your soul is to love God spiritually. It is to understand and appreciate the holiness of the One who calls us to be holy as he is holy.

Christ calls us to love God with all of our mind. It is interesting that this is not part of the famous *sh'ma* of the Old Testament. Every Jew repeated Deuteronomy 6:4-5 day after day after day: "Hear, O Israel: the LORD our God is one LORD: And thou shalt love the LORD thy God with all thine heart, and with all thy soul, and with all thy might." Jesus added a phrase that is not in Deuteronomy 6—"with all of your mind." That is very significant, especially in light of the substantial segment of the population that believes that becoming a Christian involves committing some sort of intellectual hari-kari, parking your brain in the vestibule before you enter.

Jesus Christ, the founder of the Christian faith, said that we should love God with all of our minds! Some of the greatest minds the world has ever known have been those who trusted in Christ and loved God in that way. We need to study his Word; we need to study the world that he has created; with our mind's eye we need to see God in everything. If we just stopped to realize what God has done, we would love him more, but most people walk ignorantly through life, unaware of God's many blessings.

How many people ever stop to think about how precarious our world is? Molten metal with a thin hard crust. If you reduced the earth to the size of an apple, the solid dirt we walk on would be about as thick as the apple's skin. That thin skin of dirt and cold rock is what is keeping us from being boiled alive in lava. Above us a thin layer of ozone is keeping us from being broiled by ultraviolet radiation. Is it a coincidence that both of these protective layers are in place? Or is it the providential care of God? As we use our minds to see these things, we can come to a greater appreciation of the wonder and power and omniscience of our God.

How many people ever stop to think that most liquids freeze at their densest point, but not water. What does that mean? That frozen water (ice) floats. If ice didn't float, our rivers and streams and oceans would freeze from the bottom up. Fish life would be destroyed. These and other natural phenomena show God's careful creative handiwork. As we better understand and appreciate the goodness of God, we can better love him with the mind that he has given us.

LOVING GOD WITH ALL YOUR STRENGTH

"And with all of thy strength." A love that originates in the heart, is purified in the spirit, passes through the perception of the mind, finally comes out in the strength of our arms as we serve God. Too many people in the churches around our land do little if anything in the way of serving God. If you go to church week after week and suppose that simply attending a worship service is serving God, you might as well expect a soldier to get the distinguished service cross for simply being faithful at mess. They do not give out medals for simply coming to feed your soul or your body.

People who do nothing month after month and year after year are patently breaking the first and greatest commandment in that they are not serving God; they are not loving God with all of their strength.

Who can forget the poignant line of the song—"He ain't heavy. He's my brother"? That is a service of love. If we love Christ, if we love God, we will serve him. I am afraid that many who do serve God do not prefer his service as much as they endure his service. It is not something that comes from the heart.

What is your motive for doing whatever you are doing for Jesus Christ in your church? I would urge you to ask yourself, "Am I doing this because I love God?"

A TEST OF LOVE

How can you know if you really love God? One test would be the same as it is in human relationships; if you love someone, you prefer that person's company above all else. Do you love God?

When a young man and woman fall in love, it can take a crowbar to keep them apart. It's kind of refreshing to see that young, vibrant love. If you love God, you will seek him. You will seek him in prayer; you will seek him in his Word; you will seek him in worship. I think of that great scientist and inventor of the nineteenth century, Michael Faraday, a devout Christian who discovered electromagnetic induction, which gave us the dynamo in engines and motors of all sorts. He ushered us into the electrical age. He received ninety-two awards from different scientific societies.

One Wednesday night a great banquet was held in his honor at which he was to receive a medal from the king. The preliminary speeches went on and on. Finally when the time came for the presentation of the medal, he couldn't be found. He had slipped out because it was time for a prayer meeting. He had left because he loved God more than he valued the honor bestowed by the king.

Do you remember Jacob? "Jacob served seven years for Rachel; and they seemed unto him but a few days, for the love he had to her" (Genesis 29:20). If we examine our heart to see if we prefer his company and his service above all else, we will get some idea of whether we really love and delight in God.

You might say, "Well, I know I don't love God as I ought to. I really can't say that I'm just crazy about him. How can I love him more?" People have great difficulty loving an abstraction or a force. Love must be personalized, and that is why God has come in the person of Jesus Christ, so that we might see him and see what God is like. The only begotten Son has revealed the Father. God has been personalized. When we have seen him, we will notice that there is something altogether lovely about him.

There must be something attractive in the one we love, because essentially love is the perception of some sort of excellence. Jesus Christ—the personification, the embodiment of God himself, the incarnation of God, the altogether lovely one, the most desirable person who ever lived, the friend that sticks closer than a brother, the fairest of ten thousand, the lily of the valley, the one who constantly went about doing good....

Fix your gaze on Jesus Christ—the Bridegroom—and his love for you, his bride. Let his look of love kindle in your heart and spirit a greater love for God. Let your love for him lead you to the assurance that he is utterly trustworthy.

"Thou shalt love the Lord thy God with all thy heart, and with all thy soul, and with all thy mind. This is the first and great commandment."

FOR REFLECTION

Do you really love God with all of your heart and all of your soul, with all of your mind and all of your strength?

Can you repeat the little girl's response? "But, Mommy, I am just crazy about him already!"

As you read the words of this old gospel song by Frederick Whitfield, pray that God will quicken your spirit to prefer his presence more than anything else in your life.

There is a name I love to hear,
I love to sing its worth;
It sounds like music in mine ear,
The sweetest name on earth.

Oh, how I love Jesus,
Oh, how I love Jesus,
Oh, how I love Jesus,
Because He first loved me!

FOUR

How to Trust God

Be careful for nothing; but in every thing by prayer and supplication with thanksgiving let your requests be made known unto God. Philippians 4:6

THIS EARTH is a vast theater erected by divine wisdom to be the scene of a great experiment—not an experiment in chemistry or physics or mechanics, but an experiment of far greater importance: an experiment in morality, an experiment of the spirit. This Christian view of the world and the universe is not expressed in terms of energy, matter, and force, but in terms of mind, will, and spirit.

We live in a moral universe. To fail to grasp this truth is to see the universe simply as a vast grist mill and humanity as a blind horse, dumbly staggering around on an endless circular track. The God of love has placed us in a huge treasure house filled with all manner of precious minerals, jewels, and supplies for our every need.

The real question is not "How do you find the oil buried beneath the surface?" It is "How do we use that oil?" It is not "How do we find the platinum?" It is "What do we do with it after we have found it?" It is not "How much gold can we extract from the earth?" It is "How do we use it when we have obtained it?" It is not "How finely can we grind lenses so we can search the galaxies, measure the stars, and track the comets?" It is "Behind the stars and the firmament do we see the will and the intelligence that created it all?"

This picture, this world and life view, is portrayed throughout the Scripture. In the history of Israel it is painted for us almost like a child's picture book. These lessons are written large, painted in broad strokes on the canvas of history, with an entire nation used as a brush. Everywhere you look in the history of the Israelites you find these moral lessons painted by God. You can see a picture of redemption in the Israelites' deliverance from slavery in Egypt, representing the bondage of this world, the bondage of the task master, Pharaoh—or Satan. There's the Passover night—the blood on the doorposts, the angel of death. There's the flight—the spreading of the Red Sea, the pursuit of the Egyptians, and their destruction. There's the wandering in the wilderness, the manna from heaven, the water out of the rock, the bitter water, the great test at Kadesh-barnea, the giants in the land, the crossing of the Jordan River. There's the conquest of Canaan, the embattlement of Jericho and the crumbling of its walls, the failure at Ai. Everywhere, on every page, these lessons are written large for our understanding.

In all the history of the Israelites, God was trying to teach them one great lesson. And in the New Testament it clearly states that the lesson is also for us. The tragic thing is that, despite the vast curriculum, it seems an overwhelming number of people, even in the church, have not learned the lesson that God is teaching here.

Have you learned of it? If you don't even know what it is, you obviously have not learned it. What is the one great, overarching, overriding lesson that God is trying to teach you and me through the scriptural account and the daily events in our lives? Boiled down into its most succinct form, the lesson could be stated in just two words: Trust me.

Trust me. In every circumstance of our lives this is what God is trying to teach us. It might be in business reverses, family problems, trouble with children, trouble with parents, problems in school, or problems out of school. In everything, in all events, from the smallest to the greatest calamity, or the most heartbreaking loss, our tendency is to throw ourselves upon God in utter despair and cry out, "O God, why? Why have you allowed this to come? Lord, why have you done this?"

Sometimes in utter desperation our spirits climb up that vast staircase that leads to the throne of God. We arrive only to find the door seemingly shut against us. Though we knock against its thick steel until our knuckles are raw and we cry out, there seems to be no answer. Yet there is always one answer. If you place your ear to that door, you will hear coming from the throne room a whispered, "Trust me."

WORRY—THE OPPOSITE OF TRUST AND FAITH

Let's look at the opposite of trust, which is worry. One of the most commonplace sins is worry: the gnawing anxiety in the long hours of the night; the turning, twisting, recurring anxiety that deprives us of our sleep and causes our faces to grow haggard—the anxiety that steals our joy, that removes the lightness from our tread, that dulls our eyes, that takes away our testimony for Christ.

But what is the biblical definition of *worry*? The New Testament describes the worrying of the people of the Old Testament in blunt terms: "An evil heart of unbelief" (Hebrews 3:12). Are you a worrier? Then you have an evil heart of unbelief. Worry and trust or faith are virtual opposites. You cannot have worry and faith in the same person, about the same thing, at the same time. It is impossible. Just as you cannot have air and water in the same glass at the same time; they displace one another. You cannot worry about something and have faith about it. You cannot be filled with faith and fear at the same time.

Worry! Worry! The amazing thing about this sin is that Satan has cleverly convinced some people that it is a virtue to worry! I have had people tell me, "I am a worrier," as if this meant, "I am a perfectionist," or, "Being a worrier, I really try harder." They expect me to answer, "Well, good! Hang in there! Chew those fingernails," as if their worry were a sign of diligence. A multitude of people profess faith in Christ even as they worry. Peter Marshall said, "Lord, help us to trust Thee lest our ulcers be our badge of unbelief." Worry is the opposite of faith, and it is a sin.

A RELATIONSHIP OF TRUST

The whole Christian life—the relationship with God— begins with trusting God for something. It begins with trusting God for our salvation, even as it did with the Israelites who trusted him—and he delivered them from the bondage of Egypt. When we trust Christ, his blood is applied to our hearts, and we are redeemed.

Having received that gift of salvation—through grace, by faith—you have crossed the Red Sea and are entering into the life of Christ. At this point many people expect to find a bed of roses, when instead they begin to wander through a wilderness. Every Christian must pass through that wilderness, but it was not God's purpose or intent for us to spend forty years there. The Israelites were to go directly to the mount, receive the Ten Commandments and the instructions of God, proceed to Kadesh-barnea, and enter in and occupy the Promised Land. When the twelve spies went ahead, they reported that there were giants and walled cities in the land, that the inhabitants were greater than they could conquer. Because of their unbelief, God condemned them to wander for forty years in the wilderness. He said, "So, I swore in my wrath, They shall not enter into my rest" (Hebrews 3:11). Here the writer refers back to the "provocation" in the wilderness, which kept the Israelites from God's perfect plan of immediate rest and security in the Promised Land.

Though you have been made right with God, you may not yet have entered into the rest of God. Your heart may be in a vast wilderness—wandering because of unbelief.

TRUST—HERE AND NOW

Many people who receive eternal life through faith in Christ never learn to trust Christ for the temporal things of this life. We say, "Oh, I believe God. I believe that when I step out of this world he is going to take me into everlasting mansions." But if we can't believe that God can take care of us for the next six months, how can we believe that God can take care of us forever?

From analyzing his mountains of mail, a nationally known minister with a syndicated column in hundreds of newspapers across the country says that people are concerned with two main problems: fear and worry.

But it doesn't have to be that way. The book *Hudson Taylor's Spiritual Secret* tells the story of a life lived with all the trappings taken away. Hudson Taylor, the great missionary to China and founder of the China Inland Mission, learned a great and simple spiritual secret: Just as he had trusted Christ and his promises for eternal life through faith, he could also by faith claim the promises of God and find the rest of God right here in this life.

While at school studying medicine, preparing to be a missionary, he gave away everything he had. He said, "Lord, give me this day my daily bread." God supplied his daily needs—and even more. But Hudson gave away what he didn't need. He started every day with absolutely nothing but faith and the promises of God—to supply all of his needs through Christ Jesus his Lord. During week after week, month after month, and year after year of preparation, he found that God was absolutely trustworthy. As an alien Caucasian entering into the heartland of China, he had no human friend or ally on which to depend; he simply trusted God, who provided the needs of each day. This was his spiritual secret—the secret of learning to trust Christ for the temporal things of life.

Most of us are more apt to work like this: We trust in God for our financial well-being and God blesses us. Then we take the money and invest it, and before long we are trusting in our investments. We lose sight of God.

STANDING ON THE PROMISES

Whatever trials come—whether it is a business reversal, the stock market going down, a sales contract folding, an "impossible" husband or wife, a bottle of chocolate milk dropped all over the floor—do we see these as testings from the Lord? Do we see these as places to claim his promises and learn to rest in Christ and find that he will supply everything we need?

Maybe you haven't even learned his promises, so you don't think you have anything to claim! You are like a drowning person without even a straw to claim and grab hold of. That is why you need to learn his promises and then claim them by faith. Do so and God will bring you to a place of rest and peace so you can go forward, trusting him in everything. This is what it is all about. If you haven't learned this lesson, listen to what Christ is saying: "Trust me."

Let's look at one promise: "Prove me now herewith," saith the Lord, "Bring ye all the tithes into the storehouse, that there may be meat in mine house, and prove me now herewith, saith the LORD of hosts, if I will not open you the windows of heaven, and pour you out a blessing, that there shall be not room enough to receive it" (Malachi 3:10).

A family in our church told me how they had learned to tithe and had increased their offerings above the tithe. God had blessed them! The husband said, "This year we are giving twice as much as I made five years ago." He told how God had opened the windows of heaven and poured out blessings upon them. "I don't see how God can do it. Just innumerable coincidences," he continued.

My family tried the same thing. I was challenged, some years ago, by a man who said he had increasingly given a larger percentage of his income to the Lord's work. We began to increase the amount we were giving and finally got to the place where we gave away our whole salary. All that the church gave us as a salary, we gave back. "Impossible," you say? "You can't live on air."

We don't. God opens the windows of heaven and pours out blessing upon us from all sorts of unexpected places. God just causes it to come. Some people say, "Well, you can do that because God has blessed you." No. They have the whole thing backwards. God has blessed us because we gave and trusted him. God will never be put into anyone's debt. We can prove God when he says that we are to bring all of the tithes and offerings into the storehouse. "Prove me now herewith"—this verse in Malachi is the only place in the Scripture where God calls us to prove him. If we don't, if we are not bringing our tithes—a tenth of our income—to the Lord, we are robbing him. "Ye are cursed with a curse: for ye have robbed me, even this whole nation" (Malachi 3:9). "... ye have robbed me. But ye say, Wherein have we robbed thee? In tithes and offerings" (Malachi 3:8).

Do you think that the Lord can cause your business to dry up? Do you think he can cause it be to blessed? Do you think he can bring sources of income from out of nowhere, such as you have never dreamed of? Do you? He can! I know that it is true if we trust him.

All sorts of trials and tests come, and we can't see how God is going to work out this or that. But if we could see the out-working, we would not be walking in faith. "Now faith is the substance of things hoped for, the evidence of things not seen" (Hebrews 11:1).

Trust him in adversity and in prosperity, in recession and in inflation, in sickness and in health; trust him for and in your job; trust him for finances; trust him for health; trust him for your family; trust him for your well-being; trust him for your future; trust him for the forgiving of your past; trust him for the present. In all things, at all times and in all circumstances, God is trying to teach us one lesson. "Trust me."

TRUST AND REJOICE

"Be careful for nothing"; the Bible says, "but in every thing by prayer and supplication with thanksgiving let your requests be made known unto God" (Philippians 4:6).

How can you tell whether you have faith or fear? Do you want a test? Let me give you a spiritual thermometer to place under your tongue. Be quiet. Rest your spirit a minute. If you have faith instead of worry, you will "register" a spirit of rejoicing and thanksgiving.

"Be careful for nothing." That is, be full of care and anxiety for nothing, "but in every thing by prayer and supplication with thanksgiving let your requests be known unto God." Thanksgiving and rejoicing and praise of God do not exist in the midst of worry and fear. In the same passage, Paul says, "Rejoice in the Lord alway: and again I say, Rejoice" (Philippians 4:4). How did your thermometer register? What fills your heart? Fear and anxiety and worry or faith?

And a few paragraphs later Paul gives a promise that includes a glimpse of the treasures that are ours: "But my God shall supply all your need according to his riches in glory by Christ Jesus" (Philippians 4:19). With the riches in glory as the "bank" against which we are drawing, we have reason to trust.

Remember the lesson: "Trust me." Only then can we enter into the joy of his rest, the riches of his kingdom, the delight of a close relationship with him.

As we continue to consider our relationship with him, let's look to the authority of his written Word to us. How trustworthy is the Word of God?

FOR REFLECTION

In what area of your life do you find it most difficult to turn away from fear and worry and trust God?

When your mind turns to worrisome thoughts, turn to Philippians 4:8-9 and meditate on these words:

Finally, brethren, whatsoever things are true, whatsoever things are honest, whatsoever things are just, whatsoever things are pure, whatsoever things are lovely, whatsoever things are of good report; if there be any virtue, and if there be any praise, think on these things. Those things, which ye have both learned, and received, and heard, and seen in me, do: and the God of peace shall be with you.

FIVE

How to Know that the Bible Is God's Word

All scripture is given by inspiration of God, and is profitable for doctrine, for reproof, for correction, for instruction in righteousness. 2 Timothy 3:16

THE BIBLE is the most astonishing and incredible book in the entire history of the human race. And Christians have always believed that it was the Word of God. This amazing book has been published in more editions, printed in more versions, translated into more languages, distributed more widely, than any other book in history. Well over nine billion copies of the Bible have been printed and distributed. That's almost two for every person presently upon the face of the earth!

Yet many people right here in America have no idea how remarkable and astonishing this book is. The scriptural ignorance in our country today is profound and lamentable.

But how do we know that the Bible is God's Word? Around the world twenty-six so-called scriptures are claimed to be, by their followers, words from God. So how can we know that the Bible is indeed God's Word?

Charles Wesley, the famous hymn writer, said that the Scriptures obviously were written by good men and angels or by bad men and demons or by God.

Considering those options, he concluded that the Bible could not have been written by merely good men or angels. Why? Because the Old Testament alone more than 2,600 times claims that it was written by God; it is inconceivable that good men could lie about the same subject 2,600 times ("Thus saith the Lord"; "Thus saith God Almighty"; "There came the Word of God unto the prophets saying...").

Could the Scriptures have been written by bad men? Again, Wesley thought it inconceivable to suppose that bad men or demons authored a book that claims to lift humanity and that historically has done so to the highest level of morality and purity; a book that demands the most exacting standards of righteousness and proclaims upon all sinners a most dreadful doom. Would bad men write a book that declares that all liars shall have their part in the lake of fire? No, Wesley said, concluding that the only alternative was that the book was written by God.

God himself gives other criteria for telling how we may know whether a book or prophet has come from him. Deuteronomy 18:22 says that you will know that a prophet has come from God if the things the prophet foretells come to pass. God is the only one who knows the future. "... I am God... Declaring the end from the beginning, and from ancient times the things that are not yet done..." (Isaiah 46:9b, 10a).

As one historian says, "The future turns on too many slippery ball-bearings for any human being to be able to know it." The truth of that statement is seen in the ludicrous attempts by modern prophets, seers, and psychics to "proclaim the future"; they usually get little, if anything, right.

SPECIFIC DESCRIPTIVE PROPHECIES

None of the other so-called scriptures of the world contain specific predictive prophecies—only the Bible. The Old Testament alone contains more than two thousand specific predictive prophecies that have already been fulfilled. Here is described the entire future of the great cities with which Israel had dealings. Here the future of nations is laid out so that any high school student with an encyclopedia could ascertain its truthfulness.

For example, more than one hundred specific predictive prophecies concern the great city of Babylon, including the prediction that the wall of Babylon would be destroyed and never be built again; that the mighty city of Babylon would be destroyed and never be inhabited again. Such prophecies were unheard of and such calamities were unknown, for every great destroyed city had been built again on top of the ruins of its predecessor. But here are these bold and astounding assertions of the Scripture.

The Scripture says that Babylon shall become pools of water and also that Babylon shall become as a desert. It would seem that these contradictory prophecies could not both come true. Yet travelers and explorers tell us that during some months of the year Babylon is as dry as the desert; at other times the Euphrates overflows its banks, filling the land with pools and lakes. In an incredible way, the prophecy was fulfilled. These and some one hundred more predictions about Babylon have already been fulfilled, and the test of time and the passing of centuries has failed to discount them.

Concerning Jesus Christ, more than three hundred and thirty-three specific predictive prophecies describe every detail of his life. Keep in mind that Nostradamus made a great reputation for himself, principally concerning one supposed prophecy regarding the rise of Hitler. He even got the name wrong, calling him Hisler. But he didn't designate exactly where or when he would live.

And yet these prophecies concerning Jesus Christ give the exact date when he would come into the world (see Daniel 9); the exact place: Bethlehem Ephrathah (see Micah 5:2); the incredible nature of his birth; that he would be born of a virgin (see Isaiah 7:14). All the details of his ministry and his career—his character, his betrayal for thirty pieces of silver, his crucifixion, the piercing of his hands and feet, his burial in the grave of a rich man, his resurrection from the dead, his ascension into heaven, his proclamation to the Gentiles—these and hundreds of other particulars are specifically set forth in the Old Testament prophecies. There is nothing at all in the history of literature that even vaguely approaches this sort of thing.

THE UNITY OF THE SCRIPTURE

There is a second evidence of the divine authorship of the Scripture: the amazing unity of the book—something most people would overlook. But stop and think. The Bible is composed of sixty-six different chapters or books written by about forty different authors who lived on several different continents, in numerous different nations, such as Palestine, Babylonia, Greece, Rome, Asia Minor, and perhaps Arabia. They were written by people who lived some sixty centuries apart! Yet one golden theme runs through all of these books—the golden thread of the redemption of sinful humanity by the grace of God through faith in the shed blood of the Redeemer.

Now keep in mind that there was no publisher who commissioned the writing of such a book; no editor gave forth a plan; no editorial committee oversaw its development; there was no outline distributed to the different authors. Yet from Genesis to Revelation—throughout books of prose and poetry; history and law; biography and travel; genealogies, theologies, and philosophies—an incredible unity stands.

Compare this to a painting. Suppose that forty different artists were to paint a section of a picture without having any idea what the others might be doing—or that others were doing anything at all. Yet someone collects these pieces and arranges them on a huge wall, and the result is a tremendous picture that delineates all of the features of Jesus Christ. Absolutely incredible!

Or suppose that forty different artists, without any knowledge of what the others are doing, decide to make a piece of sculpture. Yet when the pieces are glued together, it makes a beautiful statue of Christ. Beyond comprehension!

No other book in all of the world has ever been made in this way. Having written a number of books, I know what publishers and editors and editorial committees do to polish words and rearrange text. None of this was involved. And yet we have this incredibly unified book that testifies that the hand that made this book is divine.

INDESTRUCTIBILITY OF SCRIPTURE

The divine authorship of the Bible is further seen in the indestructibility of Scripture. No other book in history has endured such continued attack by so many, for so many ages. For 2,600 years all of the powers of this world have combined to destroy the Bible, and yet it remains. The anvil stands; the hammers lie broken about it.

As one person said, the Bible is somewhat like an Irishman's wall. One Irishman built a wall four feet high and five feet thick around his farm. Someone asked why he made it so thick. He replied, "If anyone knocks it over, it will be higher than it was before." Now this doesn't prove that the Bible was written by an Irishman (as sad as that may seem for a Kennedy!), but it does illustrate the remarkable and indestructible nature of the Word.

Wicked King Manasseh of Judah, born in 697 B.C., was such a violent, ungodly pagan that he determined to destroy all of the copies of the Mosaic Law, which denounced activities he was involved in—all manner of abominations, including the sacrifice of children to a pagan god. Manasseh succeeded in destroying all of the copies of the books of Moses—except the one somebody hid in the wall of the temple!

Twenty years after Manasseh's death, his grandson Josiah ascended to the throne and discovered that one copy of the Mosaic Law, the contents of which had almost been forgotten. Josiah proclaimed that the scroll be read, and that all Israel should gather together to hear the reading. The result was a tremendous religious revival among the Israelites. Indeed, the "Irishman's wall" had been turned over and found to be taller than before!

During the intertestamental period between Malachi and Matthew, Antiochus Epiphanes, a wicked Syrian tyrant, conquered Israel. He offered a pig on the altar of the temple and murdered all of those who owned a Scripture scroll. The result? The Maccabean revolt. No sooner was Antiochus in his grave than there was a great revival of interest in the Scriptures; numerous scrolls were copied.

In the Christian era, in A.D. 303, Emperor Diocletian, one of the last great Roman persecutors of the church, saw the Bible as the inspiration for the Christians' courage in opposing his paganism. He ordered the confiscation of all Christian property and the destruction and burning of all Scriptures. In ten years Diocletian was dead and Constantine the Great—a Christian— sat on the throne of Rome. Constantine not only ordered the writing of many copies of the Scripture, but he also encouraged everyone in the Roman Empire to read the Christian Bible. Again, the "Irishman's wall" "fell" higher.

During the Enlightenment, Voltaire, the famous French skeptic who so viciously attacked the Scriptures all of his life, prophesied that a hundred years after his death the Bible would be gone and forgotten, found only in some musty and dusty old bookshelf. Yet immediately after his death his printing press was used to print Bibles! His house in Geneva was bought by the Genevan Bible Society and used for the distribution of Scripture.

In more recent times higher critics have done their best to destroy the Scriptures from within. And yet never has an elephant labored longer to produce a mouse; all their efforts seem to confirm the historicity and truthfulness of the Bible.

CONFIRMATION BY ARCHAEOLOGY

Divine authorship of the Scriptures is also confirmed by archaeology, one of the wonders of our time. For the last one hundred and fifty years, archaeologists have traversed the biblical lands, many times with hostile intent and with great animosity toward the Scripture, attempting to disprove it. Yet every time they turned over their spades, it seemed they discovered another confirmation of the Scripture.

For example, the Hittite Empire, mentioned some forty

times in Genesis and other parts of the Old Testament, is not mentioned anywhere in all of secular literature. This led critics to believe that the Bible must be wrong. This must be one of the mythological peoples of the dream world of the Bible, they said. And yet today archaeology has uncovered the great Hittite Empire, giving us innumerable details about it.

Or take the case of Assyria. A hundred years ago almost nobody outside of biblical circles believed that Assyria ever existed. Again, there was not one single secular reference to the great empire of Assyria—another of the "mythological" empires of the Bible. Then a man went and did some digging! He uncovered a brick that had on it the name of Sargon, whom the Bible says was a king of Nineveh, the capital of Assyria. He sent it to scholars in Paris, who examined it and reached this profound conclusion: Since Nineveh was supposedly the capital of Assyria, and Sargon, the supposed king of this land, and since Assyria never existed, obviously this was a fraud! And yet our intrepid discoverer had the temerity to go ahead and uncover the whole city of Nineveh, including the city's great library that contained tens of thousands of cylinders and tablets giving the entire history of the great empire of Assyria, including the exploits of King Sargon.

Where are the biblical critics now? William F. Albright, famed archaeologist of Johns Hopkins University, has said that archaeology has substantially attested the entire historicity of the Old Testament tradition.

Nelson Glueck, another famed archaeologist, said that not one single archaeological discovery has ever controverted the biblical text. The more we learn about the people and the times that the Bible describes, the more we see that it is in fact true.

THE SCRIPTURE'S TRANSFORMING POWER

The divine authorship and steadfastness of the Scripture is also evident in its transforming power. The Bible says that it will transform believing nations and peoples.

I think of the famous story of *Mutiny on the Bounty*, a book and a motion picture but also based in history. But the end of the real story does not appear in the motion picture. As you know, the sailors on *HMS Bounty* mutinied and went ashore on one of the South Sea islands. Then some of them decided to leave the island before the British found them and hanged them. They took some of the native women and sailed to another island, where they soon began fighting among themselves for the women and for the few possessions they had. It seemed that the entire colony would destroy itself by murder and mayhem. But one man discovered a Bible in one of the great casks brought from the ship. As he read it, he was transformed. As he read it to others, the whole colony was changed!

Years later British forces discovered these renegades living on this island. But they had produced such a model society based upon the teachings of the Scriptures, that the government dropped all charges against them. That's the transforming power of the written Word of God.

THE WORK OF THE HOLY SPIRIT

Ultimately, the divine authority of Scripture is experienced in the human heart, in the laboratory of the human soul, by personal and intimate experience with the Author of the Scripture, the Holy Spirit. When the Holy Spirit comes to take up his residence in the human heart, people come to know that the Bible indeed is the Word of the living God.

As a young man I invited Jesus Christ to come into my life when I heard the Word of his glorious grace. He changed my life. A person who had no interest in Scripture suddenly found a hunger for it.

Many people are not interested in the Word of God. They are not interested in going to church. Why? Because they have never been changed by the Spirit of God. They do not know God; they are strangers and aliens to his kingdom; they are dead in their transgressions and sins; they are yet under condemnation, on their way to eternal death.

If you have come to know Christ, then his Spirit has come into your life. He has given you a hungering and a thirsting for his Word.

These and many other evidences demonstrate that the Scriptures are indeed the very Word of God—his Word to draw us into a relationship with himself, his Word to instruct us as we walk in the center of his will.

Ah, the evidence is there—the evidence that "All scripture is given by inspiration of God…" (2 Timothy 3:16). Yet its authority still must be accepted by faith. The problem is that sinfulness draws us away from God, even as his Spirit draws us to him.

Second Timothy 3:16 continues. If all Scripture is given by inspiration of God, then it is "profitable for doctrine, for reproof, for correction, for instruction in righteousness."

Believing that the Scriptures speak with authority does us no good if we do not read them, study them, mark them—eager to make God's words a part of the very fabric of our lives.

FOR REFLECTION

Scan the subheadings in this chapter. Ask yourself, what are the main arguments for the authenticity and inerrancy of Scripture as God's Word? How does the material presented help you better understand the authority of the Scriptures? Spend some time in reflection on these questions and decide to take seriously the role of Scripture as the Word of God in your life.

SIX

How to Study the Bible

Study to shew thyself approved unto God, a workman that needeth not to be ashamed, rightly dividing the word of truth. 2 Timothy 2:15

H E WEIGHED two hundred and forty pounds, and he had a suitcase in each hand. He was running up the stairs of the station to catch a train. By the time he reached the top, his heart almost failed him, and he had to sit down. Later, he realized he had almost caught a train without even having purchased a ticket! But he made a decision right there. He decided he had to lose weight. He had to get rid of all that excess baggage. Result: He lost sixty some pounds and was in better shape than he had been in twenty-five years. He said that the most difficult thing of all was making the decision—determining that this was what he was going to do. After that, he said, it was all downhill.

That is the way it is with most things in the moral and spiritual realm, as well. The most important thing is making up our minds that we are going to do something. That is also very true about the study of God's Word.

A recent survey by the George Gallup organization revealed that 89 percent of the people in this country *do not read the Bible daily.* That means only 11 percent do. Have you made a decision to give yourself daily to systematic and in-depth Bible study?

REASONS FOR STUDYING GOD'S WORD

Why should a person determine to study God's Word daily? I would like to suggest two reasons.

Earthly blessings. First, unless we read the Bible daily, our life here in this world is not going to be successful. I think I can state that categorically. Apart from the guidance and strength of the Word of God, your life here in this world will not be a success. You say, "My life is already a success, and I don't read the Word of God. I've got a large house, two cars and a boat, a cabin in the mountains. My life is preeminently successful." If that in essence is your answer, you don't even know what success is because you haven't been reading the Word of God. He who made your life and will judge its success or failure said this: "A man's life consisteth not in the abundance of the things which he possesseth" (Luke 12:15).

We may make a worldly show, but our life nevertheless in the end will be a failure—a dismal and gloomy failure—because we are aiming in the wrong direction. Even if we determine what the right direction is and get enough guidance from the Scripture to head in that direction, without the daily cleansing and power of the Word of God, we will not have the strength to stay on course because sin will creep into our lives.

Our relationship with God will be strained, as we turn our attention to other priorities. And the foundations of our material life will crumble. The marriage will come apart; the children will be naughty; the husband and wife will have problems. Apart from God's Word, things just will not be what they should and could be.

God's Word is a love letter that should be scrutinized. What's more, to ignore it demonstrates to our Beloved our lack of love. We cannot say that we love God and ignore his Word, his love letter to us.

It is also his last will and testament to us. Apart from the reading and claiming of the provisions of this will, we do not inherit the promises. This will is similar to God's promise to the children of Israel as they entered the Promised Land after wandering in the desert: any land on which their feet would tread he had already given to them. But they had to walk on it and claim it for their own.

So it is with the Word of God. There are thousands of promises in that Word. Promises for well-being. Promises for an intimate relationship with God. For many people they are like checks on the bank of heaven that have never been claimed. Your life will not be a success here in this world without the Word of God. With God's Word, wherever you are, your life can be preeminently successful. Whoever you are, with whatever talents you have, God can make your life richer by the reading of his Word. You must determine to pour that Word into your heart and mind until it cleanses you and strengthens you and guides you in the center of God's will.

Dr. Howard A. Kelly was one of the greatest men in the world in the early part of this century—one of the most famous medical doctors in America. His opinions were highly prized by doctors throughout the world. He wrote more than twenty books and five hundred scientific articles. To what did he owe his success? He said that he owed it to his study of the Word of God, which had made him who he was. His habits of reading the Word of God and the power and influence that he wielded as a result were legendary in his own time. He said this in his 1925 book, *A Scientific Man and the Bible* concerning his habits of reading the Word of God:

I rise regularly at six in the morning and after dressing give all of the time until our eight o'clock breakfast to the study of the Word. I find time for brief studies throughout the day and again in the evening. I make it a general rule to touch nothing but the Bible after the evening meal. It is the greatest possible help to me in my own spiritual life and growth.[1]

You wonder why your life may not be crowned with such notable success? Do you give yourself to the in-depth study of the Word of God in any way comparable to Dr. Kelly?

Heavenly blessings. The second reason you ought to study the Bible diligently is because your life hereafter will be greatly diminished by the failure to do so. Sometimes Christians forget that God has promised rewards to Christians in the future life; in heaven there are differences in degree of rewards. Those who turn many to righteousness will shine as the stars of the firmament forever. There are numerous other rewards that God has promised to his own. But those rewards only come to those who study the Word of God and who apply its principles and precepts to their lives. To the degree that you fail to read the Word of God now, you will fail to receive rewards later on.

Many suppose that they are somehow getting the best of God if they just squeak through the door of the kingdom and give little of their time or effort to God and his purposes. They do not realize that they will be the loser—both here and eternally.

In this world we humans are very aware of the differences in standing among people; we are often envious of those who are greatly blessed or highly stationed. In heaven you will wish that you were one of those who had been faithful here and had sought God's blessings. Your eternal station in heaven will be affected by your faithfulness in reading the Word of God. If you are not regularly reading and studying the Word of God, you are not experiencing what God would have for your life; you are not enjoying the fullness of an intimate relationship with him.

HINDRANCES TO DAILY BIBLE READING

What are the hindrances that keep people from diligently giving themselves to Bible study?

Haven't I read this before? A person does not read many books three or four or five or even ten or twenty—much less fifty or a hundred—times. People sometimes have the feeling, "Ho-hum, I've read this before, and I know how it's going to come out. I've heard this story; I've heard this parable; I've read this book many times."

Now the problem is that these people are used to doing nothing more than "strip mining." They just turn up the surface of the ground. They think that they have exhausted the treasures and do not know that the Bible is an inexhaustible mine of treasures. The problem is not with the Scriptures; the problem is with them. They do not dig deeper to find the treasure that God has for them. They give little effort, make cursory attempts at reading the Scriptures, and find that they get little out of it. Little given gives little in return.

I just can't understand this. Often, people repeatedly and endlessly read certain passages that they feel they can understand; then they ignore large sections of Scripture that they find difficult.

Yes, some portions of the Bible are very difficult to understand, but sometimes an in-depth study of those passages will yield great rewards. How many times have you struggled through the "begats" and wondered why in the world God ever put these into the Bible? I remember three Jewish men who were converted to Christ. When asked what Bible passages had the greatest impact upon them in their conversion, they replied, "The genealogies in Matthew and in Luke—the begats." There they saw the tracing of the Messiah back to Abraham and David.

In Acts 8 Philip came upon an Ethiopian eunuch who was reading a passage from the prophet Isaiah. Philip said to him, "Understandest thou what thou readest?" And he said, "How can I, except some man should guide me?" (vv. 30-31). Philip stepped in and provided instruction. Today there are numerous written helps available, and I think we can have our own private, portable Philip at our side to help us daily in the understanding of the Word.

HOW TO MAKE BIBLE STUDY PROFITABLE

If Bible study is profitable, it will be enjoyable and it will be fun. How can this be done? Again, I have two points.

Find and learn how to use available helps and tools. Every Christian ought to take advantage of some of the study helps so readily available to us here in America.

Some of these tools are not the cheapest of books. On the other hand, how many of you have garages that are loaded with electric saws, hammers, wrenches, screwdrivers, and all sorts of other gadgets? Of course, everybody knows that a house is more important than a soul. Or is it? Soon the house will turn to ashes, but the soul will outlast the stars. I think that the maintenance of a soul is vastly more important than the maintenance of a house. And yet many people would spend far more on tools for the latter than for the former.

What tools are critically helpful to Bible study?

First I would mention a complete concordance—a book that contains every word found in the Scripture and the references for where that word is cited. If you know any word of any verse in the Bible, you can find where that verse is, or you can find verses on a particular subject. Probably the two most popular concordances are *Young's Analytical Concordance* to the Bible and *Strong's Exhaustive Concordance*. Someone has said, "Young for the young and Strong for the stronger Christian." Either one of these is an outstanding biblical aid, and every Christian should have one.

Second, a Bible dictionary can be a great help in understanding many of the terms in the Bible. Of the dictionaries available I would recommend either *Davis Dictionary of the Bible* (Broadman, 1954) or *The New Bible Dictionary* edited by J.D. Douglas (Tyndale, 1982). Both are excellent Bible dictionaries that will be a great source of understanding and illumination of the Scripture.

A third important tool is a commentary, which gives a passage of Scripture and then explains what it means. Hundreds and hundreds of commentaries are available, but if I had to recommend one, it would be the one by Matthew Henry. This classic of devotional commentary on the Scripture has stood the test of time and led thousands of people to a closer relationship with God. Charles Spurgeon, the great preacher of England, said he used to read it continually. George Whitefield, largely responsible along with Jonathan Edwards for the Great Awakening here in America in the eighteenth century, said that he had read the entire six volumes of *Matthew Henry* through four times.

Many other tools can be a great help to you in the study of the Word of God, but these are three of the most basic ones.

HOW TO STUDY A PASSAGE

How do we go about studying the Bible?

Reading. Obviously, the first method is simply to read it. Dr. Kelly said,

And now for my greatest secret for everyday common folks, known through the ages and yet ever needing to be restated and learned afresh as generation succeeds generation. It is this. The very best way to study the Bible is simply to read it daily with close attention and with prayer to see the light that shines from its pages, to meditate upon it, and to continue to read until somehow it works itself, its words, its expressions, its teachings, its habits of thought, and its presentation of God and His Christ into the very warp and woof of one's being.[2]

No, there is nothing remarkable about that, it is wonderfully simple. But it works.

Perhaps you have been reading the Bible but would like something a little bit more challenging, or a little bit more exciting. There are many other ways.

Mastering a book. The second method is to master a book of the Bible. In this case you take a smaller portion of Scripture and determine not just to skim across its surface but to dig down, to mine some of the treasures that are there. For instance, say you were to study the books of 1 Kings and 2 Kings. These books record the age of Solomon and then all of the history of the divided kingdom under the nineteen kings of Israel and the nineteen kings and one queen of Judah, and all of their doings and the results. Many people pass over this portion of Scripture without even reading, because they feel it is much too complicated.

But if you were to really dig into it, you might memorize the names of all those kings, find out who they were and the relationships that they had to one another. You'd be amazed at all you might learn in such a study.

Mastering a character. A third method is the study of the various Bible characters. The Bible is a book about life and about living beings, and we can learn a great deal from it. People study life because they live and they are interested in living and in other people. The lives of great people challenge us to the possibilities of our own existence. Someone said that every Christian should claim a particular individual as his or her "own," finding out everything he or she can about this person—and God will reward this effort greatly.

Noted Bible scholar, Dr. Wilbur Smith, in *Profitable Bible Study*, gives some suggestions for this sort of study and some pitfalls to avoid. He says, "Collect all of the material which the Bible contains on one character that you would like to study. But in doing so, be sure you are not gathering material about two or more different persons of the same name."[3]

Did you know that there are thirty characters in the Old Testament named Zechariah? That there are fifteen Old Testament characters named Jonathan? There are twenty characters by the name of Nathan. In the New Testament are eight characters by the name of Judas. An interesting study would be to find out who these people are and what can be learned about them. There are seven women named Mary in the New Testament; five different men called James; five called John. Some Bible characters even have more than one name. For example, Simon is also called Peter; he is also called Cephas and Barjonah. A Bible dictionary would be helpful here.

Gather together material on one character, find out about that person's parents, childhood influences, and so forth. What was the one great outstanding virtue of this person? (Do you have an outstanding virtue?) What was his or her weakness? What sin perhaps brought about the destruction of his or her life? (Do you have such a besetting sin?) What were the influences that led to its development? What were the temptations that led to its exercise? What were the results that followed from its transgressions? What effect did this person have upon others? What influence for good or for evil did he or she exercise? What can you learn from looking at this life? This method provides a very interesting study from the Word of God.

Studying a word, name, place, or subject. Another method is to study the words of Scripture. The Bible is the Word of God and it contains the words of God. There are some six thousand different English words in the Old and New Testaments, many of which will reward you greatly if you study them. Take, for example, the word *gift*. Do you know that the Scripture mentions almost three hundred gifts that God gives to us? Or make a study of the names of God. God is called *Jehovah-tsidkenu*, "The Lord Is Our Righteousness"; in his righteousness we are clothed to stand faultless before God. He is called *Jehovah-jireh*, the name given to God by Abraham at Mount Moriah when God provided the sacrifice and freed Isaac. The name means "The Lord Will Provide." Another name is *Jehovah-shalom*, "The Lord Is Our Peace." In this age of anxiety, it is good to know that our peace is to be found in Jehovah, in the living God, revealed in Jesus Christ.

A study could be made of the names of Jesus, as hundreds are given to Christ throughout the Old and New Testaments.

The geography of the Holy Land and surrounding countries will greatly illumine the whole story of the Bible. Follow Paul's journeys or the travels of the people of Israel.

There are almost two thousand biblical prophecies already fulfilled; these make a fascinating study.

Would you like to learn to pray better? Make a special study of the prayers of the Bible and what those prayers teach us about praying.

Studying Jesus. Most of all, we need to study the person of Christ as he is revealed. He is the great central personage of the revelation of God. Someone once took the Constitution of the United States and wrote it all out in longhand. As you read it, you see just the words of the document. But if you move back away from it, you get another picture—a beautiful portrait of George Washington made as some of the strokes of the letters are darker than others. It was a magnificent work of art.

So it is with the Bible. At first you may see only stories about seemingly unrelated things, but after a while you will see that all of Scripture points to Jesus Christ, the Lord of glory. The Old Testament foretells his coming; the Gospels describe that he has come; the Epistles explain why he came. It is a picture of Jesus Christ that should be the center of all of our study. And that picture leads us to a deeper relationship with him.

Imagine visiting in the home of some friends of yours back during the Desert Storm operation in the Persian Gulf. The husband, John, has gone overseas to fight in the war. He is advancing through the sands of Iraq, fighting Saddam Hussein's elite Republican Guard, and wondering if any mine fields lie ahead. Perhaps he is seriously wounded, his life in danger. And so you say to Mary, "Mary, how is John doing? What do you hear from him?"

She says, "Oh, I'm so glad you mentioned John. You know, I love John more than anything in this world. He is the very apple of my eye, the delight of my life. He fills my heart. He is my all in all."

"Well, how is he doing, Mary?"

"I really don't know."

"Oh, you haven't heard from him?"

"Well, yes, I have. In fact, that stack of letters there on the coffee table is all from John, but I just haven't had the time to read them. You know, these have been such busy days. There's my job, and then, of course, there are the tennis lessons and time on the golf course. There's so much to do at the house, too. I've been meaning to read those letters one of these days, but I just haven't had the time yet. Someday I'm sure I will because I just love John with all my heart."

It doesn't add up, does it? That's not how it works. Yet perhaps on your coffee table, or somewhere in your house, there are sixty-six love letters from God. You profess in word and song to believe in him and to love him, but you just don't have the time to read his letters to you.

Every Christian wanting an intimate relationship with God needs to make a decision—to read and study God's Word daily. By that Word we delight in God and he delights in us. By that Word our lives will bring upon our own heads the rewards that God offers so graciously to those who will seek and honor him. By that Word we live the kind of a life that will make us a success here and a good influence upon those with whom we live.

FOR REFLECTION

Is Bible reading and study a top priority in your daily schedule? If not, what changes do you need to make? What tools or helps might make your Bible study more enlightening?

Stop right now and talk to God. Confess any hypocrisy that has hindered your relationship with him. Ask for his empowering strength to help you stay on the path—at the center of his will. Ask that he open your eyes to insights he wants to give you as you read on—considering your own maturity in Christ.

Part Two

Your Maturity in Christ

SEVEN

How to Know You Have Been Born Again

Jesus answered and said unto him, Verily, verily, I say unto thee, Except a man be born again, he cannot see the kingdom of God. John 3:3

MATURING IN CHRIST. Where does the process begin? When we are born again and first enter into the kingdom of God. After that momentous event we need to grow in Christ; we need to live out the life to which God calls his children. In earlier chapters we've detailed the "how-to" of being justified by faith and growing in your personal relationship with God. In this chapter we'll begin to look at the personal maturity and growth that comes as a result of being born anew of the Spirit.

According to a Gallup poll, four in ten Americans claim to have been "born again." Yet when you look at the morality of some of these people, you can't help but question whether or not they have any real idea of what the term even means. The secular media tends to trivialize or mock Christian expressions. That is certainly what has happened to the term *born again*. In fact, one survey indicated that a large number of people thought that Jimmy

Carter first used the phrase *born again*—an indication of the abject spiritual ignorance of our day.

From the way the media has trivialized this term, many people really don't know what it means at all. I read about a "born again" baseball team; it had come out of a slump! There is a song that refers to the thrill of looking into a love's eyes and being born again. Then there was a cover of *Time* magazine some years ago when Bjorn Borg won his fourth Wimbledon title. They featured his picture with the caption "Bjorn Again."

Of course the source of this term was not Jimmy Carter; it was Jesus Christ who made it perfectly clear when he said emphatically to Nicodemus that unless a person be born again it is not even remotely possible for him or her to see the kingdom of God, much less enter therein. "... Ye must be born again" (John 3:7).

A new preacher came to a church and the first Sunday morning preached on the subject "Ye Must Be Born Again." And the people listened with interest. The following Sunday he preached on the subject "Ye Must Be Born Again." The following week he again preached on the subject "Ye *Must* Be Born Again," at which time one of his parishioners came up and said, "Preacher, why is it that you keep preaching on the subject "Ye Must Be Born Again"? The preacher replied: "Because ye must."

Some people suppose that born-again Christians are some sect that came into existence in the last twenty years. Of course, the very phrase *born-again Christian* is a redundancy, since there is no such thing as a non-born-again Christian and there is no such thing as a born-again non-Christian. Every true Christian is born again.

Many people don't realize that all historic Christian denominations have always held that a new birth is essential to enter into salvation. That is a view not only of Presbyterians and Methodists and Lutherans and Baptists and Congregationalists and Episcopalians but also of Roman Catholics and Greek Orthodox. There is no Christian denomination that does not maintain that this is true.

But tragically millions of people in our country and even in our churches have no experiential knowledge of what it means to be born again.

The Bible makes it very clear that we should examine ourselves to see if we be in the faith. "Let no man deceive himself" (1 Corinthians 3:18a). "Be not deceived," Paul writes repeatedly. It is quite possible and common for people to deceive themselves; they will substitute something far less for that life-transforming experience without which one shall not see paradise.

So I urge you today to examine yourself to see if you truly have been born anew. Imagine the tragedy, the ultimate and unspeakable tragedy, of waking up two minutes after death and discovering that you had deceived your own heart and found yourself in hell—forever. "Be not deceived." "Let no man deceive himself." "Examine yourselves, whether ye be in the faith" (2 Corinthians 13:5a).

What, then, are the signs of regeneration or the new birth?

A SIGN OF NEW BIRTH: SALVATION BY FAITH IN CHRIST

The first and universal sign of a spiritual new birth—and there is no exception to this—is that every single person who has been born of God will trust in Jesus Christ *alone* for salvation.

After presenting this material to a group of people, a young woman came and asked me a few questions. In return I asked a few of her: "What are you basing your hope of eternal life upon?"

She replied, "Well, upon Jesus Christ *and* my efforts to do the best I can."

I asked her if she believed that she had been born again.

She said no, but she was working toward it.

My friends, you cannot work toward it; you cannot work until you first have been born.

Regeneration is necessary for redemption, and in this a human being is ultimately passive; you and I can do nothing about it. Until we are born again we are dead in trespasses and sin. We can no more be born spiritually by ourselves than we could be born physically by ourselves. What did you have to do with being born physically into this world? Nothing! One can no more "give birth to oneself" than Lazarus could raise himself from the dead.

Salvation is of God, and only he can quicken the dead. Those who are quickened are quickened because they have looked to the Cross of Jesus Christ. They have found themselves trusting in him and have later discovered that the Spirit of God was working in their hearts. All who are born again rest their whole hope of heaven upon the Son of God who loved them, who came into this world and suffered and died in agony to pay the penalty for their sins, that they might have eternal life. Do you know that you've been born again?

SIGN OF NEW BIRTH: NEW CREATURE IN CHRIST

Second, all of those who have been born again have become new creatures in Jesus Christ. The Bible says, "Therefore, if any man be in Christ, he is a new creature; old things are passed away; behold, all things are become new" (2 Corinthians 5:17). Have you become that kind of a new creature? Has your old life passed away?

In his book *Loving God*, Chuck Colson talks about probably the most notorious gangster in America in the second half of the twentieth century: Mickey Cohen. He was an unusual character. He had a friend by the name of Bill Jones who had been involved in some unsavory things but had become a Christian. Jones shared the gospel with Mickey and asked him if he wanted to pray and accept Christ. To Jones' surprise, Mickey said yes. He prayed, and Jones rejoiced happily that this man had been converted.

But as the weeks and months went by, Mickey was spending less and less time with Bill Jones and Jim Vaus, another former gangster who had become a Christian. Mickey returned to his old mob friends. One time Jones went to Mickey and told him that as a new Christian he ought to be staying away from his unsavory friends. Mickey replied,

Jones, you never told me that I had to give up my career. You never told me that I had to give up my friends. There are Christian movie stars, Christian athletes, Christian business-men. So what's the matter with being a Christian gangster? If I have to give up all that—if that's Christianity—count me out.

Cohen wasn't willing to repent and turn from the old life and become a new creature and follow Jesus Christ.

About ten years ago the news reports said that Jimmy Carter's sister had supposedly led Larry Flynt, publisher of *Hustler* maga-zine, to Christ. Born again. It was all the talk. Well, it wasn't too long until Larry Flynt denied outright that he had been born again. It was soon very clear that he wasn't going to give up his *Hustler* empire. When he began to say all sorts of vile things about Christianity and Christians, one media wag said that Larry Flynt had now been "porn again."

Do not deceive yourselves. If you truly have been born again, you have become a new creature in Jesus Christ. Old things have passed away; what's more, all things are become new.

We are born into a new world. Even as a baby—coming forth out of the watery womb into this world of sunlight and air—must marvel at the new environment, so it is with a Chris-tian. The grass is a greener hue; the skies are a bluer blue; all things become different when we become new creatures in Jesus Christ. Our affections are changed.

I have often said that when I was born again God reached down and stuck a screwdriver in my "wanter"; he turned my "wanter" upside down! Those things I had always wanted, I didn't want anymore. Those things I had never wanted at all, I suddenly had a great desire for. God granted unto me new and holy affections. That is what it means to be born again. I ask you, my friend, have *you* been born again?

SIGN OF NEW BIRTH: LOVING CHRIST

Third, if we have been born again, we will inevitably love Jesus Christ with all of our hearts and minds; we will desire him; his desires will become our desires; his passion will become our passion; his purpose will become our purpose in life; his kingdom will become our delight; what he hates, we will hate; what he loves, we will love. We will desire to know him better; we will desire to seek him in his Word; we will desire to seek him in prayer; we will desire to seek him in worship.

Many people suppose they can be a Christian and never go to church. Let me make it very clear: Not everyone who goes to church is necessarily a Christian. But all true Christians who are physically able do go to church. It is inevitable. Why? Because they have a heart's hunger for the worship of God.

If I were to put a bowl of Gravy Train before you, you would probably gag at the sight and smell of it. It would probably take two or three strong men to force you to eat it. However, if I were to zap you with a magic wand and transform you into a cocker spaniel, all I would have to do is place the bowl in front of you—and get my fingers out of the way before you ate them too! You would have a desire for dog food because you would be a dog.

You will have a desire for spiritual food if you have become a spiritual person in Jesus Christ. Many people have all sorts of reasons why they don't go to church. I've said to a number of them, "Let me tell you. That's not the reason you don't go to church at all. The reason you don't go to church is not because you work hard all week. It's not because you want to sleep in on Sunday. It's not because you want to read the comics. The reason you don't go to church is because you have never been born again. It's just that simple, for if you had, you would. God would place the desire within your heart and you would want to do so."

SIGN OF NEW BIRTH: DESIRE TO KEEP HIS COMMANDMENTS

Fourth, a person who has been born again will desire to keep the commandments of God. Jesus Christ said, "If ye love me, keep my commandments" (John 14:15). So it becomes the Christian's joy to keep the commandments of God. For the unregenerate heart, the commandments are a great burden. But those who have been renewed in heart and spirit can say with David, "O how love I thy law!" (Psalm 119:97a). "... Thy law *is* my delight" (Psalm 119:174).

God says that he will write his laws upon the fleshly tablets of our hearts (see 2 Corinthians 3:3). Let not that immoral person who ignores the commandments of God and lives in sin and wickedness claim to have been born of God. Now a person may demonstrate an outward conformity to the commandments of God and never have experienced the transforming work of God. Someone has said, "Mere morality is perfectly consistent with a heart of unsubdued and unyielding enmity to God." But all of those who are truly Christ's will desire to live according to his commandments. All true Christians delight to follow Christ in his law.

SIGN OF NEW BIRTH: LOVE FOR FELLOW CHRISTIANS

Further, a person who has been born again will love the fellowship of believers. Jesus said, "By this shall all *men* know that ye are my disciples, if ye have love one to another" (John 13:35). This is one of the marks of the true believer. In the physical world "birds of a feather flock together." That same is true in the spiritual world. One of the ways you can tell whether or not you have been born again is very simple: Look at your friends. Are they born again? If they are not, you probably are not either.

Yes, Jesus walked among the publicans and sinners. I walk among the publicans and the sinners—the unregenerate and those whose hearts are at enmity with God. But Jesus went among them to *give* and not to get. And so do I, and so do all of those who are truly born of God. But if you find that your fellowship, your recreation, your pleasure, your enjoyable company is found among unbelievers whose hearts are unchanged, whose spirits are set against God, then ask yourself whether you are truly born of God.

SIGN OF NEW BIRTH: DESIRE TO MAKE CHRIST KNOWN

Finally, those who have been born of God desire what Christ desires: to make him known to other people. Someone well said that the Christian faith can be described in four words: admit, submit, commit, and transmit. How true that is. We must *admit* our sins. We must *submit* ourselves to the lordship of Jesus Christ. We must *commit* ourselves to his will and his kingdom. And we must *transmit* the gospel of his grace to those who live in darkness. If Jesus Christ lives his life in us, then we see through Christ's eyes; we hear through his ears; our heart feels what he feels; his passion is our passion; his concerns are our concerns.

When we look out at the world of lost men and women who are on their way to eternal perdition, who are dead in trespasses and sin and have no hope for all eternity, our hearts will break for them—even as Christ looked down on Jerusalem and said, "O Jerusalem, Jerusalem... how often would I have gathered thy children together, even as a hen gathereth her chickens under her wings, and ye would not!" (Matthew 23:37).

We will have a heartfelt concern for lost men and women, so that when we meet someone, our first thought will be this: Does this person know Jesus Christ? We cannot have faith in Jesus Christ and profess to love other people without being concerned for the eternal well-being of their souls.

You say, "Well, I'm too shy or too timid to say anything to

them." I assure you, my friend, if you walk around the block tonight and see flames leaping out of the back bedroom of a neighbor's house, you will not say to yourself, "Oh, my, that house is on fire. The people inside are probably going to be burned alive. It's too bad that I can't do anything for them, but I am so shy. I can't speak. I've never really had a course in raising an alarm. There's nothing I can do. I must go home and go to bed."

Of course not! You would cry out at the top of your voice: "Fire!" You would pound on the door until you awakened someone. But do you realize that your actions would be based upon faith and love? A faith that there is somebody in the house. You don't know if there is anybody there; they may all be away for the week. But since you believe that someone's home, you act accordingly. Now the inhabitants may indeed smell the smoke and get themselves out without your help. But you don't know that to be true, so by faith you act as if your action would be the determining factor in their living or dying. It is also based on love, because you have some concern and care for them.

So too when we know that no one shall live without Christ, how can we say that we have faith in him and then fail to share his love with others? The reality is that apart from his salvation no one has any hope beyond the grave. Those who are unregenerate and unchanged face an eternal condemnation that is beyond the ability of this teacher to explain or describe. How can we say we believe that and declare we have any love or concern for our fellow human beings and not speak to them about Christ?

If Jesus dwells in us, then his passion will be our passion; his concern will be our concern. He was always passionately concerned for one and the same thing: the eternal human soul. So I ask you again: Do you know that you have been born again? Be not deceived. Examine yourselves.

HOW TO HAVE THE ASSURANCE OF SALVATION

What must we do to be saved? The Spirit of God uses the Word of God and the gospel of Christ to affect your personal salvation. I urge you, if you do not know beyond any shadow of a doubt that you have been saved and you have been transformed, lift up your eyes to Calvary and see there the divine Son of God, the Creator of the world, dying in your place, enduring your punishment, paying for your transgressions, suffering for your sins, purchasing for you a place in paradise, and calling you to bend your knee before him. Invite him into your heart as Lord and Savior and Master; place your trust in him alone for your salvation; repent of your sins and commit yourself to him. And you will discover to your astonishment that you have been born again.

Here's how the great preacher Charles Spurgeon described the traumatic moment when he came face to face with this Savior, the hour in which he put off the old man and put on the new, the unforgettable day on which he was born all over again.

There was a day, as I took my walks, when I came hard by a spot forever engraven upon my memory, for there I saw this Friend, my best, my only Friend, murdered. I stooped down in sad affright, and looked at Him. I saw that His hands had been pierced with rough iron nails, and His feet had been rent in the same way. There was misery in His dead countenance so terrible that I scarcely dared to look upon it. His body was emaciated with hunger, His back was red with bloody scourges, and His brow had a circle of wounds about it: clearly could one see that these had been pierced by thorns. I shuddered, for I had known this Friend full well. He never had a fault; He was the purest of the pure, the holiest of the holy. Who could have injured Him? For He never injured any man: all His life long He "went about doing good"; He had healed the sick, He had fed the hungry, He had raised the dead: for which of these works did they kill Him? He had never breathed out anything else but love; and as I looked into the poor sorrowful face, so full of agony, and yet so full of love, I wondered who could have been a wretch so vile as to pierce hands like His. I said within myself, "Where can these traitors live? Who are these that could have smitten such an One as this?" Had they murdered an oppressor, we might have forgiven them; had they slain one who had indulged in vice or villainy, it might have been his desert; had it been a murderer and a rebel, or one who had committed sedition, we would have said, "Bury his corpse: justice has at last given him his due." But when Thou wast slain, my best, my only-beloved, where lodged the traitors? Let me seize them, and they shall be put to death. If there be torments that I can devise, surely they shall endure them all. Oh! what jealousy; what revenge I felt! If I might but find these murderers, what would I not do with them! And as I looked upon that corpse, I heard a footstep, and wondered where it was. I listened, and I clearly perceived that the murderer was close at hand. It was dark, and I groped about to find him. I found that, somehow or other, wherever I put out my hand, I could not meet with him, for he was nearer to me than my hand would go. At last I put my hand upon my breast. "I have thee now," said I; for lo! he was in my own heart; the murderer was hiding within my own bosom, dwelling in the recesses of my inmost soul. Ah! then I wept indeed, that I, in the very presence of my murdered Master, should be harbouring the murderer; and I felt myself most guilty while I bowed over His corpse, and sang that plaintive hymn—

"'Twas you, my sins, my cruel sins,
 His chief tormentors were;

Each of my crimes became a nail,
 And unbelief the spear."[1]

Spurgeon compares this day of new birth to all other days that are like coins worn from circulation, until the image and super-scription has been obliterated. But this one day is bright and fresh and as new as if but yesterday it had come from the mint of time.

Do you have that assurance of salvation? Do you know you've been born again?

FOR REFLECTION

Have you been born again? This is one question that no one can afford to be unsure about. Review the subheadings in this chapter. If you have any doubts about your salvation and sincerely want to be a Christian, pray, trusting in the blood of Christ, claiming God's promise to make you a new creature. Accept Jesus Christ as your Lord and Savior. Commit your life to him.

Being a new creature, you will have a new desire to be pure in heart. There will be a newness and freshness to life—a desire to love and obey God above all else.

EIGHT

How to Be Pure in Heart

Blessed are the pure in heart: for they shall see God.

Matthew 5:8

OUR AGE HAS BEEN CALLED MANY THINGS: the nuclear age, the space age, the computer age, the age of anxiety. But yet another designation is altogether fitting and proper—fitting in a way it never has been before. We can say that we live in the age of environmental hazards such as pollution—one of the hallmarks of our century. We have air pollution, water pollution, and even the ground is polluted with chemical and nuclear wastes. We have food polluted with additives and pesticides. We all know what smog is—biting and stinging, reddening the eyes.

I recall flying into one of our northern industrial cities. From the air the city looked as if it had been hit by an atomic bomb. A huge orangish cloud enveloped the skyline. I considered taking a deep breath before the plane penetrated this smoggy cloud and holding my breath until I left. I relayed my concerns to one of the city's residents, and he said, "Oh, no, that was not air pollution. You see, that was caused by the orangish lights we use to light the streets."

I said, "But you don't understand. I flew in at noon!"

We live in age of pollution. But it is also an age of "spiritual pollution." A moral smog has settled down upon civilization today. It is found in our books and magazines, our motion pictures, our television programs, and radio talk shows. It is found in our speech. It is seeping like noxious chemicals, corrupting and polluting the very moral water we drink.

When I was in New York in graduate school, a smog enveloped the city one day—a smog so dense that, though I was only two or three blocks away, I could not see the Empire State Building. Now just as a physical smog can block out something as vast as the Empire State Building, a spiritual smog—a moral smog—can block out God. It is no wonder that we live in an age of doubt, an age of unbelief, an age of skepticism, an age of atheistic humanism, because the moral fog of our time has blinded the eyes of people so that they are not able to see God.

Consider the words of our Lord: "Blessed are the pure in heart: for they shall see God." The vision is not given because of one's advanced degrees or expansive learning; it is given to those who are pure of heart, holy of life. If we would see God, then we must be like him.

THE PROMISE: SEEING GOD

The happiness of seeing God has been called the brightest star in the constellation of the Beatitudes. The mystics of the Middle Ages rejoiced in the concept of seeing God—the most blessed of all visions. They called it the Beatific Vision, and it was the great quest of theology, the great quest of piety, the great quest of philosophy. It was even the quest of science as originally construed—that through the examination of the cosmos, humanity would be drawn to see the Creator more clearly.

To see God means not merely to see him with the physical eyes—for no man can thus see God, though many have sought to do so. One of the disciples said to Jesus: "... Lord, shew us the Father, and it sufficeth us" (John 14:8).

This was true not only of the apostles, but even pagan princes have sought the same thing. A well-established legend recounts how the Emperor Trajan said to one of the believers in the true God, "I understand that you believe that your God is everywhere. And he dwells among the nations. I should very much like to see him."

To which this believer responded: "I am afraid, sire, that no mortal eye can look upon his glory and that person live for he is too glorious for the eye to behold."

"Nevertheless," said the emperor, "I am your king and I command you that you show me your God."

"Very well, sire, but before I do, I think it best that you look upon one of his ambassadors before you attempt to look him in the face."

And with that, he led Emperor Trajan outdoors on a bright and dazzling midday. He bade him to look up into the sun shining in the heavens. The emperor exclaimed, "I cannot, for the light dazzles my eyes!"

The believer said, "If you cannot look upon one of his ambassadors that carries the message of his creation to the world each day, then how shall you look into the face of God himself?"

No, the Beatific Vision does not involve seeing him with the physical eyes, but seeing him with the eyes of the soul—experiencing his joy and peace, his serenity. This is what people are really searching for in life. They are searching for peace of heart and mind; that deep abiding joy that only God can give them. This is the great quest of life in all of its parts. This is what God says we may have, but we can have it only in his way.

HIS TERMS, NOT OURS

I recall reading of an unbeliever in his mid-twenties who was troubled with the thought that there might be a God. One day as he walked out into a pine forest, his thoughts turned to questions that troubled his heart and mind: Where did I come from? Is there a God? If so, am I accountable to him? He came at last to a small sandy spot where he sat down and fixed his eye on a small pine tree.

Out loud he said, "God, if you are there, smite that tree and I will believe in you." He waited. He watched. Nothing happened.

But, you see, God is the one who sets the conditions whereby we may see him and know him. It is not up to us to dictate terms to God. In his Word he clearly says that we are to repent of our sins and trust his Son, Jesus Christ, and that by purity of heart we shall see him as he is—his glory shining forth from the face of Christ.

Some years ago I encountered a young man—a snarling skeptic—who attended the high school and college youth group I was visiting. He was a caustic unbeliever if ever there was one. I shall never forget his remarks. He said, "Why, this is nonsense! What is wrong with you people? There is no God, and I will prove it to you." He continued, "God, if you really exist, strike me dead on the spot." The group became very quiet. Nothing happened!

I chuckled and said that reminded me of a six-year-old boy going up to Mohammed Ali (who happened to be the heavyweight champion of the world at the time) and saying to him, "Mohammed Ali, you think you are big stuff, don't you? You think you are the world champion. But you are not so tough. I can take you on any day. In fact, if you want to prove that you are the world heavyweight champion, let's see you knock me down!"

I can imagine Mohammed Ali looking at him with something between a sneer and a laugh and walking away.

The little boy might then say, "You see, I proved that Mohammed Ali is not the world heavyweight champion."

Of course, he proved nothing of the sort; he merely proved that he was a fool. His challenge was utterly beneath the champion.

And so was our young skeptic's challenge completely beneath God—a God who had at one time swept the entire human race into oblivion with a flood. God will set the terms. And his terms are being pure of heart. Be like him and you shall see him. You shall also be blessed.

THE BLESSED ONES

The word *blessed*, in its deepest and most significant sense, means "happy"—not with the mere happiness of the froth of waves dashed by the wind but with a happiness that extends to the very depths of the sea. It is a deep calm, an abiding joy, an everlasting happiness; it is the joy that is at the right hand of God.

"Happy are the pure in heart," said Christ. But the world's message flies completely in the face of that word when it says: Happy are the *impure* in heart. Satan's lie is compounded: Not only are the impure in heart happy, but the more impurities and contaminants they may pour and dump into their hearts, the happier they are going to be. Happy are the exceedingly impure in heart. Happy are those who have HBO, especially late at night. Happy are those who go to R- and X-rated films. Happy are those who read *Playboy* magazine. Happy, happy, happy are those who dump impurities into their hearts. This is the great message of the world.

You see it everywhere. Dump your wife and find another and you will be happy. But it starts "smaller." You begin to think: "I cannot be put in jail for just looking—just a little impurity will make me a little bit happier." When we think that way, we do not realize that we are giving up and forsaking the greatest happiness in all the world. Do you believe Jesus Christ when he says, "Blessed [happy] are the pure in heart"?

There is a great Dutch painting that shows a little girl holding a cherished toy in her hand. But the painting also shows her dropping that toy. At first you are perplexed as to why she would let go of something so dear to her heart. But then, over on the side of the painting, you notice a pure white dove fluttering toward her open hand.

And so it is with God. He would offer the dove of peace and

love and joy, but too many people have their hands clutched tightly to some of the deceitful baubles of this world. The greatest happiness we can ever know—the happiness of seeing God—is lost through impurity of heart.

PURITY OF HEART

The terms of our seeing God are that we be pure in heart. What does that mean? The word *katharoi* (pure), in the original Greek, means that which has been cleansed; that from which the impurities have been removed.

In the *Idylls of the King* there is a story about a land that had been ravaged by wild beasts. They had slipped down out of the mountains and destroyed children and adults alike. Finally a crusade is announced and brave men take sword and spear in hand and go forth to destroy these ferocious monsters. At last the final beast is killed and, as the *Idyll* says, "the land is cleansed once more; at last it is pure."

This is an interesting use of the word *pure:* rid of wild beasts. Yet if we stop to think about it, there is a bit of the tiger in all of us. In fact, deep down in the caves and caverns of the human soul all manner of wild and ferocious creatures lurk. There is the lion of lust; the fox of deceit; the serpent of lasciviousness; the bear of boorishness; and many others in a veritable zoo that occupies the human heart. If the land is to be cleansed, if we are to be pure, then these creatures must be slain.

Another illustration of the meaning of the word *katharoi* (pure) deals with water. If water has been freed from all impurities so that it becomes clear and transparent, then that water has become pure. And so it is with our hearts. They are to be clear and clean like purified water.

Proverbs 4:23 says to "Keep thy heart with all diligence; for out of it are the issues of life." We believe that God has given us a great commission to carry the gospel to all the world. We believe that God has given us a cultural mandate to change the face of humankind, to affect the various spheres of society with the truths of the gospel. But it all begins in that citadel of the human heart. If that is impure, then we shall do very little to purify or transform our world. As Proverbs 23:7 says, "For as he [a person] thinketh in his heart, so is he...."

GUARDING THE HEART AGAINST POLLUTION

Impurities such as lust and lasciviousness are like drops of acid falling into a crystal clear chalice of water.

The corroding acid of pride as we lift ourselves up and do not call upon God or show him gratitude indeed makes cloudy the water of our hearts.

Then there is the acid of critical thoughts and critical talk. Some people cannot meet and talk with anyone about anything without finding someone to tear down or destroy. Yet each of their words is an acid that clouds the water of their hearts and prevents a clear vision of God.

There is the acid of impatience. Awhile ago I was reminded of that as I felt the drops dripping in my own soul. By nature I am a very impatient man; I want to get done and I want to do it now. But I realized that such an attitude of impatience is really a critical attitude toward other people. It is a condemning attitude toward the slow, toward those who will not get up and get going. Such an attitude of impatience deprives our hearts of any serenity or peace and any vision of God.

There is the acid of anger—the most corrosive acid, indeed. We cannot see God at all when our hearts are angry.

There is also the acid of jealousy and envy.

And then there are negative and unbelieving thoughts— doubts about what God can do for us or through us. All of these prevent us from seeing God. They prevent us from the joy, peace, love, and serenity that Christ would give to us.

In a world sinking in a moral morass, there is a tremendous need for purity. How beautiful is that single white flower that blooms in the midst of a black, dank swamp. How beautiful is the true life that is given over to holiness and purity, that is determined not to be a part of the corrupted and polluted world in which we live. It is a life that will see God.

When he was eighteen years old, Jonathan Edwards, a great preacher of the eighteenth century, wrote these words: "If there could be one man in the world at one time who was pleasing to God, I would want to be that man." One man in the whole world pleasing to God! One shining white flower in the midst of a black swamp! Did he succeed? Jonathan Edwards became the greatest, the most original philosopher in the history of America. All of his writings were recently reproduced by the Yale Department of Philosophy. Furthermore, his sermons were very influential in the Great Awakening that transformed New England and led the way to the American Revolution. One man, pleasing to God, had an enormous impact upon his culture and his society.

Said James the brother of Christ: "Purify your hearts, ye double minded" (James 4:8). My friend, too many people claim to be believers in Jesus Christ; they try to hold onto Christ and the things of his church, and at the same time they are trying to get a little happiness into their lives as they imbibe a little bit of the world. They do not realize that they are destroying the very happiness they seek.

Happy are the pure in heart. Oh, that we would believe that truth and stop the lie. "How?" you ask. It seems that what I have described is a Mount Everest rising up into the sky, miles above you, with white snow shining in the sun. But you are down in the lowlands with noxious fumes swirling about you, your feet stuck in the mud. How can you ascend?

"What can wash away sin? Nothing but the blood of Jesus," says the old song. The blood of Jesus Christ can purify our hearts. One drop of that blood can turn the most polluted chalice into crystal clear water. If you feel that your heart is polluted and corrupted with sin, then ask Christ to cleanse you, to make you pure within. Then ask that by the power of his Spirit he would give you the desire—that holy desire—to keep your heart, to guard your heart, to watch it each day, to keep it pure that you might ever see that vision of Christ; that you might be that one person—even the only one—in all the world, whose chief and greatest desire in life is to please God.

You shall discover that the pure of heart are mature at heart. You shall discover that which the world vainly seeks after and shall never find. You shall discover that true happiness comes to the pure in heart as you see and experience God himself. You shall discover how to receive the richness of God's blessings.

FOR REFLECTION

Prayerfully consider and list any habitual thoughts, words, and actions that are clouding the water of your life. Take this list to God and ask for his grace and his strength. Ask him to help you mature in Christ so that you might know the happiness of seeing him.

NINE

How to Receive God's Blessings

Resist the devil, and he will flee from you. Draw nigh to God, and he will draw nigh to you. Cleanse your hands, ye sinners; and purify your hearts, ye double minded.

James 4:7b-8

"OH, WHAT A FOOL I WAS!" Driving along in the car to an early morning appointment, the gentleman with me uttered those exclamatory words. He went on to tell an interesting story. For a number of years he had desperately wanted two things: to be reconciled to a person very dear to him and from whom he was estranged; to make a decent living from his business, which was a continuing struggle.

Now, for the past three weeks, he had attended a church prayer meeting every morning, and he couldn't believe what had happened in his life! The estranged person's heart had been changed; he knew God was at work in that situation. He also had made more money in the last three weeks than in any three-week period in his life; his heart was filled with joy.

"Oh, what a fool I was not to realize!" said he. Realize what? The truth of the words of James 4:8: "Draw nigh to God, and he will draw nigh to you." And James 4:2: "Ye fight and war, yet ye have not, because ye ask not."

There is a great principle and question involved here. We are such needy creatures, you and I. We are creatures but of the moment. Our lives are like the grass that grows up in the morning and in the afternoon is cut down, like the vapor that arises up and then is blown away. Yet even during that brief space of time while we walk upon this earth, before that hour comes when others shall walk upon us, our lives are filled with needs. We are so finite and so needy. All of these needs clamor within us and cry out to be filled. One of the greatest questions of life is this: What will meet the needs of my life? Where will I find the satisfaction of all of these needs that cry out within me?

ON WHOM DO YOU RELY?

Basically, there are only two answers to that question, and your heart is going to come down on one or the other. You are either going to learn that the answer to your needs is in God—the Giver of every good and perfect gift (see James 1:17), the One in whom we live and move and have our being (see Acts 17:28), the One who has given us life and all things to enjoy, the One who is the source of every blessing—or else you are going to place your confidence in something else. And it really makes very little difference what that something else is.

If you have turned from the living God, you are resting your strength upon a broken reed. Whether you are trusting, as most humanists today do, in yourself and your own confidence, whether you say that there is no deity to save us and that we must save ourselves and provide the solution to our own problems, whether you turn to some false god or false cult, whether you turn to the state as the answer to your needs, or whether you make a compact with the devil, ultimately in every case you are resting your hopes upon a lie. You are trusting in precisely what Satan wants you to trust in because he does care what you call it as long as it is not God in Jesus Christ.

FLEE THE DEVIL, LOOK TO GOD WITH CONFIDENCE

I would remind you that Satan pays very poor wages. He does not even respect the minimum wage law. He promises much, but he gives very little. Sin has its pleasure for a season, but all too soon the season is over, the pleasure is gone, the tide is out, and you are left high and dry. The promise is great, but when you approach the paymaster and ask for your pay, though you may see all manner of precious goodies waiting for you, when you reach out your hand, you are grasped and led away by demonic forces. There you face the grave; you are cast in among the cackling of demons, and the bottom of that grave opens up to drop you into the blackness of hell. The wages of sin are death and destruction.

God is the giver of every good and perfect gift. James says that we are to resist Satan, and he will flee from us. We are also to draw nigh to God. As we do so, he will draw nigh to us.

Let me repeat this again: Draw nigh to God. I am afraid that too many people look upon religion as a burden to be borne—not as a power to bear them up. They look upon it as some sort of a curse that they have to drag along behind them like an iron chain, rather than looking upon it as the source of every blessing. How do you see it? Do you see the commandments of God as something chafing, something restricting, something narrowing? If so, you have believed the first lie of Satan who convinced Eve that God was a cosmic killjoy. Or have you seen God as the source of all real joy?

It is interesting that people caught up in sin lead miserable lives. You can always tell if somebody has drawn nigh to God; at that person's right hand there is joy forevermore! One of the greatest lies that Satan has ever told is that to be godly is to be unhappy. Remember the Prodigal Son? He wasn't rejoicing while he was in the midst of the swine, filling his belly with the husks. Rather, he found a place of rejoicing as he sat at the feast table of his father with the ring on his finger and robes on his back.

Draw nigh to God, and he will draw nigh to you in blessing. Do you really believe that? Most people probably do not. I think it is evidenced by the fact that they spend so little time drawing nigh to God. Where does it fit in your daily priorities? Yesterday where did drawing nigh to God fit into your schedule? How about the day before? Last week? Last month? If it wasn't on your schedule, it is because you have believed the lie of Satan that God is some burden that you must bear and not the source of every blessing. God desires to bless your life.

DRAW NIGH THROUGH THE WORD

How do we draw nigh to God? Unquestionably we begin to draw nigh when we take his Word seriously. He speaks to us in the Scriptures—sixty-six love letters from God. As we take him seriously, we will draw nigh through his Word.

Reading the Word. I remember one day sitting in my office, studying, when one of our staff members knocked at the door. He said, "There are half a dozen young men out here who are dressed in long white robes, and they talk funny. I think you had better come out and see them." As an aside, he said, "They are also eating the children's cookies and punch."

I went out to see what these young men might need. I discovered six of them in their early twenties. Their robes, once white, were now quite road-worn, and all of their worldly possessions were wrapped in blankets over their shoulders. I greeted them, and they greeted me, calling me "brother." We talked, and I questioned them. With evasive answers, all they told me was that they were part of "the family of God." I decided to proceed a bit further in the questioning and asked them what they thought about Jesus Christ and who he was. It became very clear that they did not know who he was and had some vague view that he was a manifestation of something or other.

Then I began to talk about salvation. Well, their view of salvation was one of human works—that by obeying certain commands, some of which they invented for themselves, they would ultimately gain entrance into heaven. They claimed to be following the teachings of Jesus, which they summed up in four things: One, don't kill anyone. Two, eat no meat. (As vegetarians they had a little problem with the fact that Jesus ate fish.) Three—no sex, whether in marriage or out (I reminded them that it was very likely that their cult would be short-lived if they stuck to that principle and also that if Adam and Eve had followed their command, none of us would have existed at all). The fourth commandment was no materialism.

As we talked, I asked them, "If you follow these commandments, will you earn your way into heaven?" I explained the doctrine of grace, but their minds were blinded. They could not understand what I was talking about when I told them that eternal life is a free gift, that they could not earn it by keeping these or any other commandments. Nor did they have the right to choose these commandments over other commandments of the Bible. If they were to get to heaven by keeping the commandments, they must keep *all* of God's commandments in heart and mind and soul *all* of the time—and no one has ever done that.

They insisted that they had and that they were perfect. I said to them, "Have you never read 1 John 8, where it says, 'If we say that we have no sin, we deceive ourselves, and the truth is not in us... If we say that we have not sinned, we make him [God] a liar, and his word is not in us'?" It appeared that they were not aware of those verses, so I continued, "May I see your Bible?"

One said that he didn't have one. I asked another, and he didn't have one. None of them had a Bible! I said, "My friends, you do err not knowing the Scriptures. You have a few texts here and there that you have taken out of context, but you do not read the Word of God." Jesus said, "Search the Scriptures...." (John 5:39). Psalm 119:11 says, "Thy Word have I hid in mine heart...." But they were ignorant of so many things, because they did not study the Word of God.

A returning missionary from Africa said that the condemnation of America may be found in the dust on the covers of our Bibles and on the stubs of our checkbooks—an indication of our worldliness.

Is the Word of God an integral part of your life? Do you love it? Do you read it? Do you desire to hear it and study it?

Hiding the Word in the heart. Some time ago I received a set of cassettes containing the entire New Testament. At the time I did not have a cassette player in my car, but now I do, and I want to tell you that I am having the greatest time with it. Though I have always hated to drive and have always hated to travel, now I get into the car, push in a cassette, and I begin to hear the Word of God. It just comes like a healing stream over my soul, and it is a blessed thing. If you don't have one, I would urge you to get one because you can have so many opportunities that you can redeem with the Word of God. It is a great way to hide the Word in your heart! How much Scripture do you have in your mind?

A local restaurant has papered the walls with old newspapers. It is interesting to read headlines and even fine print of what happened forty or fifty years ago. But it is much more wonderful to paper the walls of your mind with the Word of God—eternal truths that never go out of date. God can bless your life and draw you into spiritual maturity by calling to your remembrance the things the Holy Spirit has taught through Jesus Christ. This is where he can give guidance and knowledge and wisdom; where he can empower your life; where he can give you strength to face the challenges of life; where he can give you power to witness for Jesus Christ; where you can be filled with joy. All of this comes through his Word. If you would draw nigh unto God, you would love his Word.

DRAW NIGH IN PRAYER

Second, we draw nigh to God in prayer. That may seem self-evident. But let me ask this: Do you look upon prayer as a privilege or a burden? How do you see it? With a group of ministers I once had the pleasure of having breakfast with President Carter when he was in office. After the meeting he said something I have not forgotten. He said that if any of us had any need to contact him, he was available and could be reached at any time through his aide. I thought that was an unusual gesture for someone in his station to make.

How much more wonderful it is that the Creator and Sustainer of all of the universe, the omnipotent, omniscient God, says to us that we can come to him for any reason, at any time, with any problem. We do not have to go through an aide! We can just pick up the phone of prayer and call him directly. We will never get a busy signal and never find that no one is at home. He will always be there. And he always has the answer! What a privilege it is!

Like my friend driving the car, how many of us would have the honesty to say, "What a fool I have been!" How many things in your life have been going wrong because you haven't really been seeking God, you haven't really been drawing nigh to God? And so your life has withered like an unwatered plant, like a flower that is drying up and dying in desperation.

God, the Source of life, is willing to pour out the streams of water upon you and cause your life to blossom, to flourish, if you will but seek him. They who seek the Lord are wise. They who seek the Lord are mature. He desires to bless you if you would not just occasionally but faithfully, day after day, seek the Lord. Call upon him while he is near in prayer and in your daily life.

When you are not praying, think about him. See his handiwork in all of his creation. Praise him, day by day and hour by hour, for what he has done.

We draw nigh to God when we sing his praises! May a song of praise arise spontaneously from your heart and lips. May you see his providence and know that in everything he is at work in your life.

How wonderful to see Christians who have been strengthened by his Word and who see the hand of providence in whatever is taking place in their lives—while others go to pieces and their lives fall apart because they do not see the hand of God working his mysterious wonders.

DRAW NIGH THROUGH OBEDIENCE

We draw nigh to God also through obedience. That is why James goes on to say, "Cleanse your hands, ye sinners; and purify your hearts, ye double minded. Be afflicted, and mourn, and weep" (James 4:8-9a). We need to repent of our sins if we are to draw nigh to God. We need to walk obediently with him. Yet how often do we see obedience as a galling, chafing yoke upon our shoulders and do not see, rather, that obedience is a portal to blessings from God? How many blessings has God been ready to pour out upon your head—but you have shut off and short-circuited them by disobedience and sin and doubt that God, the source of every good and perfect gift, wants to bless your life. We have not because we ask not, and we ask and receive not because we ask amiss.

I urge you to determine above all else in your life to draw nigh to God, day by day, hour by hour—in habits of Bible study and prayer, by hiding his Word in your heart, by praising his name, by thinking about him, by obeying his commands. Walk the road of maturity in Christ, and you will see how he will send the spring rains upon your life to make it flourish and bloom.

FOR REFLECTION

Are you saying, "Oh, what a fool I was—or am"? Have you turned from your first love and lost the joy and freshness, the wonder and excitement you had when you first came to know Christ? If so, it's not that God has turned away from you. It is sin and doubt entering into your life that has caused you to turn away from the Lord—who eagerly desires to delight in your presence.

God waits for you. He does more than that. Like the father of the Prodigal Son, seeing you from afar, he wants to run to greet you and welcome you, exchanging your rags for robes.

Hear his promise: "Draw nigh to me, and I will draw nigh to you"—to forgive you, to cleanse you, to renew you, to give you life eternal, and to make your life right here and now what I would have it to be. He has a more wonderful plan than you have ever dreamed possible.

TEN

How to Be Successful God's Way

... seek ye first the kingdom of God, and his righteousness; and all these things shall be added unto you. Matthew 6:33

THE TIME: 5:17 IN THE MORNING, July 17, 1938. The place: a small airport in New York City located near where Kennedy Airport stands today. The person: a thirty-one-year-old pilot who had just set a new speed record traveling from Long Beach, California to New York City. This young man named Douglas was preparing to return to California. He loaded his plane with three hundred and twenty gallons of fuel, several quarts of oil, and a large supply of Fig Newtons. After a long taxi down the runway, the plane finally lifted up, into the air, moving off into the distance. But the startled ground crew stood helpless as they saw the plane slowly arc out over the Atlantic and disappear eastward into a dense fog that had moved in.

Twenty-four hours later our intrepid pilot saw the fog beneath him disperse; to his amazement, when he looked down, he saw stone houses with thatched roofs, arranged on streets of cobblestone. He knew something was wrong. He found an airport and landed. When a group of men greeted him with thick Irish brogues, he knew he was in Dublin, not California! He explained rather blithely, "I guess I just flew the wrong way." So Douglas Corrigan had his name once and forever changed to "Wrong-way" Corrigan.

When he returned home, he discovered to his astonishment that he was a national hero—the center attraction at a ticker tape parade. He was publicly congratulated—for who knows what—by the U.S. Ambassador to Great Britain, Joseph Kennedy. To make the ridiculous absurd, they went on to make a motion picture about the misadventures of "Wrong-way" Corrigan, from which this fifty-dollar-a-week mechanic-pilot made some seventy-five thousand dollars. It seems to me that there has to be a lesson in all of that.

LESSON FROM THE GRIDIRON

Maybe old "Wrong-way" can teach us something. If he cannot, then let me give an illustration from a football game. Another true story: an eager player scooped up a fumbled ball. Evading several tacklers who spun him first this way and then the other, he kept running. He stiff-armed a couple more, leaped over another, and finally broke into the open field. As the goal posts loomed before him, he appeared to be setting a new record for open field running. The crowd in the stands leaped to its feet with a gigantic roar. He looked behind him and saw both teams in hot pursuit, but no one could catch him now. Worst of all, he couldn't hear the shouts of his own teammates yelling, "You're going the wrong way!"

After he crossed the goal line, smashing the ball on the ground and leaping up into the air, he suddenly was utterly devastated when his teammates finally got through to him. He had gone the wrong way and lost the game.

In the midst of the roar of the crowd, many people don't hear the voice of Jesus saying, "You're going the wrong way!" The indispensable factor for success is that we set out for the right goal. Nothing else will suffice. It matters not that our intrepid football player was able to shake off several tacklers, that his knees were pumping in the classic textbook style, that his stiff-arm was perhaps the finest ever to be seen, that he twisted and turned and leaped and sped as no other runner ever had breaking into the open. All that meant absolutely nothing when it was discovered, too late, that he had been going the wrong way.

Our class or distinction in life, our cabinets full of awards and trophies, will mean absolutely nothing if we learn, all too late, that we have been going the wrong way.

The incredible story of "Wrong-way" Corrigan teaches that the world may applaud us even while we are going the wrong way. The world might hold a parade for us. We might be congratulated by dignitaries. We might achieve fame because a motion picture about our life is created. We might even come into considerable money. Yes, we might end up wealthy and famous and cheered by all only to discover, too late, that we had been going the wrong way.

Many other factors are involved in success: motivation and visualization and imagination and application and perseverance, but before any of these, and essential to all of them, is that we select the right goal—the choice to go the right way.

In our football illustration another player on the team may have gone only five yards and not fifty or sixty or seventy. But going five yards in the right direction would have been better than running ninety-five in the wrong direction. The world is filled with people who have accomplished amazing things, only to discover, too late, that they were going the wrong way.

DANGEROUS DETOURS

How are we to be successful? How are we to find the right goal? We need to be aware of some of the wrong goals that we select too often. We allow the world to set the agenda for us, to define the terms, to establish the goals toward which we are heading. We are like little toy soldiers that a boy turns around and marches up a board. We start out in the direction in which we have been turned. Surely the vast majority of church members have allowed the directions of their lives to be determined not by the Word of God but by the world.

Let's look at some false goals.

The goal of riches. A young man told me that when he was in college a few years ago he asked some of his fellow students what their major was.

They said, "Accounting."

He asked, "You like figures?"

Several of them replied, "No. Not particularly."

"Well, why are you majoring in accounting?"

They replied, "That is where the jobs are. That's where you can really make some money."

The young man perceived that it was strange for people to spend most of their waking hours working on a job they dislike just to make some money in order to make themselves rich. They would spend most of their lives in misery—to make themselves rich and supposedly happy and secure. It seems like a foolish thing to do, yet millions of people do it. They work in jobs they do not like. Some of you reading this book don't like your jobs at all. Some of you hate them, yet you let the world set the agenda for you. A few years ago a popular book was titled *How to Think and Grow Rich*. But for a Christian, getting rich is a totally improper goal. The idea that a Christian should set riches as a life goal is totally contrary to the Scripture.

God may be pleased to make you rich. There is nothing wrong with riches in themselves. There is something definitely wrong with seeking them. As Paul says, "For the love of money is the root of all evil..." (1 Timothy 6:10).

Of all the goals I have ever sought in life, I don't believe I have sought either for money or for any tangible earthly goal. God has been pleased to bless me with many earthly things, but I have never sought them. Jesus made it very clear that we are not to have earthly goals. I bristle when I hear of various motivation clinics that encourage people to strive for what *they* want, to seek out an abundance of earthly goods. Go for that new Cadillac, they would say.

But that is not what Christ said. If you believe such bunk, you are letting the world set the agenda for your life. Your life will ultimately become a failure. The world may applaud you and honor you for running after the things of this world, but when you cross the goal line, there will be weeping and wailing and gnashing of teeth.

My young friend thought it was strange that people would work in accounting even though they didn't like it. He said, "They ought to choose, if they are going to have the proper idea of success, a job they like, a job that makes them happy."

The goal of earthly happiness. That brings us to a second idea frequently set before Americans today: Being happy is a key goal in life. Success means being happy more than it means being right. People are looking for just a little happiness. That may sound nice to you, but Scripture affirms that happiness is not the goal of our lives. Jesus said that we are to seek the kingdom of God and not to seek after happiness.

An interesting thing about happiness is that those who *seek* happiness seldom find it. Happiness is a by-product of seeking something higher than yourself. Seeking your own happiness is totally selfish. No, happiness is not the intended result of a successful life.

The goal of self-realization. Success is often measured by the development of a person's talents and potentialities, so self-realization has been advanced as yet another goal. Of course we ought to develop our minds and our bodies and our talents. But for what purpose and with what motives?

I have talked to people who told me they were "getting in shape." There is nothing wrong with getting in shape, but I have asked a number of them, "Getting in shape for what?"

Nobody I've asked has been able to answer that. What are we getting in shape for? What is the purpose for which we are getting and staying in shape? Getting in shape is not a goal in itself.

The goal of applause. Some measure success by fame, the applause of others. If they can go down in history as one of the hundred or two hundred or one thousand famous people, then they will have been successful. However, the applause of men and women is very fickle. Those who cheer one day may boo the next. Those who were saying, "Hallelujah," to the Son of David on Palm Sunday were saying, "Away with him; crucify him," a few days later. When the lid has finally been lowered onto the coffin, the applause of others will mean nothing at all.

If we are going to consider what real success is, we must identify and define it. Strangely enough, the books on success I read in preparation for this topic reported various methods for reaching success, but they did not say what success meant. At best, they described it in ambiguous terms.

SEEKING FIRST THE KINGDOM

If we are going to be successful, we need to understand what is meant by success. Jesus described it for us in the Sermon on the Mount. He said, "Seek ye first the kingdom of God, and his righteousness, and all these things shall be added unto you" (Matthew 6:33). Interestingly, those who seek the will of God, who seek his kingdom, are usually those who find that God blesses them. Those things that others spend their life seeking but never really finding are given to them by God. "For after all these things [food, drink, clothing—material possessions] do the Gentiles seek," Jesus said in Matthew 6:32. Here "Gentiles" is simply another word for "heathen." Sadly, there are church members who fit into this category. Jesus said their lives would be failures. Christ must set the agenda; Christ must define the terms; Christ must establish the goal. Ultimately, his Word will determine whether we were a failure or a success.

If the whole world applauds but Christ says nay, then one's life is a tragic failure.

If you are a Christian, you are in some sense seeking the kingdom of God. Yet Charles Spurgeon once said cogently, "The Bible never tells us to seek the kingdom of God; it tells us to seek it first." So to the four preceding wrong views of success to which most of you might say, "Well, that doesn't quite describe me," I would like to add a fifth, which will include a vastly larger group of people: a wrong goal in life is to seek the kingdom of God with anything less than your whole heart, soul, mind, and strength. Do not be deceived, for Christ said, "Seek ye *first* the kingdom of God, and his righteousness; and all these things shall be added unto you."

At various points in the Sermon on the Mount, Jesus was refuting the teaching of the scribes and Pharisees. But at this point there is no refutation of any teaching of theirs. He launches out on his own, out into the deep, and this teaching is peculiarly Christ's. It is the secret of Christ, of his guidance to us for a successful life, of his revealing the secret of what will make our lives successes or failures.

I have never forgotten the words missionary and explorer David Livingstone wrote in his diary after suffering incredible hardships and personal loss, "My Jesus, my Christ, my God, my King, my All, I again consecrate my life entirely unto Thee. I will place no value upon any thing or any relationship except as it relates to Thy Kingdom and Thy cause." A great hero of faith, Livingstone opened up Africa to the gospel, bringing it to millions of people who had never heard it before. His words and actions exemplify what it means to seek first the kingdom of Christ—to be a success.

What are *you* seeking first in your life? Have you let the world turn you around and point you off in its own direction? Are you a "Wrong-way" Corrigan, a confused football player running in the wrong direction on your way toward ultimate disappointment and failure? Or have you come to understand the truth that Christ would have us know?

Jesus Christ was the great example of one who sought the

kingdom of God with everything he had. His whole life was devoted to doing his Father's will, "... I come to do thy will, O God..." (Hebrews 10:9). That he purposed as the goal of his life; that reality he lived every single day of his life.

My friend, I hope you will take his goal as your own. Unless you do, in the end you will discover that you have gone the wrong way. And you will discover you are really miserable and not at all happy and pleased with yourself.

How can you be successful? Christ makes it very simple. He takes that which most people place as subordinate and places it in the premier position: "Seek ye *first* the kingdom of God, and his righteousness."

As you put his kingdom first all these things—success and maturity in Christ—will be yours. Go for it!

FOR REFLECTION

Which of the "wrong-way" goals is most tempting to you?

Is the question "What can I do for the kingdom of God today?" part of your wake-up routine? Many of you go month after month and year after year without ever asking yourself that question in the morning. It is not the goal of your life. It is not the intention of your heart. You are not seeking first the kingdom of God.

I urge you, ask the question now. Ask it tomorrow morning and the next morning. Let the Lord of your life set your goals and direct your paths.

Do so and you will be on the right path—rejoicing all the way.

ELEVEN

How to Rejoice in Any Circumstance

This is the day which the LORD hath made; we will rejoice and be glad in it. Psalm 118:24

W HEN THE LORD called Adoniram Judson to Burma, no missionary had ever settled among the enigmatic, mysterious people of that land. Judson's heart pulsed with joy, anticipating sharing the gospel with them for the first time. He could hardly contain himself throughout the long voyage across the ocean.

At last ashore in Burma, Judson determined to leap over the one obstacle to his purpose: language. He spoke no Burmese and the Burmese spoke no English. Regardless of this, he hurried down the street until he saw a Burmese man.

Since the Burmese considered it impolite to stare at other people, this pedestrian cast a glance in Judson's direction but quickly turned away. Yet he felt drawn to look back because of the glow on Judson's face, which was all teeth and smiles and sparkling eyes. Judson looked ready to jump into the air and click his heels at any moment.

Turning away again, the Burmese fellow sensed motion

coming toward him. Sure enough, his downward gaze saw the foreigner's feet coming closer. The man then jerked his head up, dropped his mouth open, and widened his eyes, for Judson was rushing right at him until he was enveloped in a big bearish hug. He heard excited utterances in some strange, unintelligible tongue. Then the beaming Judson practically bounded away—down the street. The astonished Burmese went home and told his family he had just met an angel whose out-of-this-world joy had bubbled up and spilled out in the form of a warm, hearty hug. Such was the joy of Adoniram Judson.

And such an other-worldly joy can spill forth from the life of a mature believer—walking in the center of God's will.

WHY WE HAVE HAPPINESS

Some people complain that Jesus did not exude the joy he has given to others. They view Christ as a cosmic killjoy with nothing better to do than throw a wet blanket over all the felicities of life. Yet though Jesus was "... a man of sorrows, and acquainted with grief..." (Isaiah 53:3), and we read no Scripture that tells of his laughter, our understanding of the great work he accomplished must delve further to see the superficiality of such a conclusion.

Jesus entered this world and gathered unto himself all our sins, all our guilt, all our woes, all our sorrows, all our sicknesses. He lifted them up with himself when that cursed cross was raised up against the gray Judean sky, so that we, now unburdened, now unchained, might receive his heavenly joy.

Jesus knew the hypocrites of his time, and of times to come, would disfigure their faces and wear sad countenances to show off a godly spirit (see Matthew 6:16). He warned against such a pretense. Instead, he admonished his followers to rejoice and be glad.

We need to remember Satan's first and greatest and most successful lie: "I want you to be glad, but God wants you to be sad." That is Satan's basic propaganda. He says it over and over a thousand times in a thousand different ways. Remember what he said to Eve? "Did God tell you not to eat of the fruit of that tree? Why, God knows that you are going to be like gods if you eat that fruit; that is, your life is going to be expanded and enriched, and you are going to be happy and full of joy" (see Genesis 3). Eve believed the lie; she ate; she died.

That is what Satan has been saying ever since. "God," he says in effect, "wants you to have those things that look bad and taste bitter, and certainly they are going to make you appear stupid. The whole world is going to laugh at you, if you get tied up in this religious thing. But I (Satan) want you to have that which really looks sharp and tastes delicious and is going to make you bright and with it, if you will just forget this old fuddy-duddy idea about God." Have you ever believed that lie? I think all of us have fallen prey to it at one time or another. According to him, God wants us to be sad. Satan wants us to be happy, to be glad!

Telling from the expressions on their faces and their attitudes, many church members spend most of their lives in an attempt to confirm the truthfulness of that lie. They seem bent on testifying to the truthfulness of the father of lies. How about you? What is your face testifying to? A face that is completely relaxed is a smiling face. (That is why a corpse smiles.) How much effort does it take for your countenance to smile?

TRUE HAPPINESS IS BLIND TO EXTERNAL STIMULI

Because so many people are looking for happiness, dozens of books have attempted to define it and prescribe a method for its acquisition. You may have read some of those books—good for a few laughs: *Happiness Is a Fuzzy Kitten; Happiness Is a Little Puppy; Happiness Is Watching Your Boss Slip on a Banana Peel.*

Almost all the *Happiness Is...* books of a few years back tell us that some event or circumstance external to the human person produces happiness. They are wide of the mark. However, one book does hit the bull's-eye. I will share with you God's counsel on happiness, so that if you have been experiencing a bare minimum of it—or less than your heart yearns for—you can hear the Word and seize the opportunity to improve the character of your life by putting God's Word into practice.

It has been said that happiness is the flag that flies from the castle of your heart when the King is in residence there.[1] When this ideal is working in our lives, external events or circumstances no longer determine whether or not we are going to be happy. Happiness is an internal affair not dependent on external stimuli. For example, the authorities in Philippi had Paul and Silas scourged, imprisoned, and bound in stocks. In spite of this, Paul and Silas found the joy within themselves to sing praises to the Lord, a happiness the people who placed them there did not possess (see Acts 16).

Paul and Silas could sing praises in a dungeon, yet today's elite, who possess all the gadgets and comforts and material security that the mass of ordinary people think would "buy" happiness, often seem quite miserable in the midst of their wealth.

Happiness is a state of mind that does not depend on external things. If we do rely on external events and circumstances going just right, our happiness will be fleeting.

The next time you go to England, visit Middlehum Castle, an ancient fortress that has withstood many a siege. You must pass through an outer wall and fortifications, then through an inner wall and fortifications before you can stand before the castle itself. From there, two more formidable walls surround the inner sanctum where the inhabitants lived. There in the center is a deep well from which they drew fresh, clear water—water that made them independent from any external source and able to withstand long sieges. That is a beautiful picture of what God wants our lives to be like. Jesus Christ said his Spirit would be as a well of water in us, springing up into eternal life, bubbling and sparkling and bringing joy (see John 4:14)—even if there are "hostile armies" outside the wall. The Christian can withstand any siege!

HAPPINESS IS A CHOICE

The second thing we need to realize is that we choose to be happy or not. Happiness is an act of the will.

Most of us grow up thinking that we experience something and then respond by being happy or unhappy. What makes me happy? That choo-choo train. My new sports car. That new, expensive dress would make me happy. What makes me unhappy? No dessert after dinner. The delivery boy forgetting to leave the morning paper. Having to watch five little monsters while the wife spends the day at Neiman-Marcus with all my credit cards. Whatever the case, the idea is that we passively receive some experience that activates happiness or unhappiness in us.

The Bible says that this idea is false. We have the choice of being happy or not. Does Psalm 118:24 read, "This is the day which the Lord hath made. May something come along that will make me happy in it"? No, it doesn't. Yet how many of us face the new day with that modification of Scripture in mind? The text reads, "This is the day which the LORD hath made; we will rejoice and be glad in it!" Note that we are to rejoice and then be glad. In psychology it is known that inward feelings often follow outward actions.

THE COMMAND TO BE HAPPY

Paul instructs, "Rejoice in the Lord always..." (Philippians 4:4). That is an imperative, not a good wish. He continues, "And again I say unto you, rejoice." This is a command of God. The Greek word is *chairoie*, which means "rejoice, be glad, leap with joy, sing aloud." When is the last time you leaped for joy?

If we do not execute the command to rejoice, we are disobeying God. If we are disobeying God, we are sinning. Those who wear a long face and turned-down mouth are Benedict Arnolds in God's kingdom. They advertise the devil's propaganda that Jesus is a killjoy rather than the King of joy. A Christian most convincingly attests a personal faith by rejoicing.

There once was a bigoted Chinese man who lived next door to a missionary. Knowing nothing about this Christian religion except that it was foreign, he would have nothing to do with it. He refused to speak to his Christian neighbor about it or to let his neighbor speak to him about it.

Nonetheless, after some years the Chinese man walked over to his Christian neighbor's house and said, "I don't know anything about your religion, and I really don't want to hear about it, but over the years I have heard the laughter that so often rises from your house through your windows. I have heard the singing and laughing from the houses of my countrymen who have embraced this religion. I have said to myself that if there is something that gives such joy, I would like to know what it is."

Robert Louis Stevenson appreciated people who had joy and happiness and who showed it. He said, "You know, when a happy person walks into a room, it is just like somebody has lighted another candle." Such a person is a benediction to your life. Do you know anybody like that? Would a stranger take you for a Christian by the happy look on your face? Does your home sing with the joy of the Lord Jesus?

YOU CAN OPT FOR HAPPINESS

You can make a choice to be happy; happiness is an act of the will. But what do these statements mean?

The faculty of the seminary I attended was divided. Not all professors devoted themselves to teaching their students the historic Christian faith. Some men of radical theological persuasion fostered skepticism and even unbelief. I challenged one such professor in class one day concerning a part of the Old Testament, but he retorted vigorously, "You do not understand. What I am telling you is what the scholars say."

I was taken aback. I thought I might well be wrong—if the scholars who had looked into this matter at great depth were agreed. Even worse, maybe the Bible was wrong. So I visited an old professor who believed the historic Christian faith—a brilliant scholar himself. I related what had happened and finished by saying, "My professor said that such was what the scholars believed. Is that true?"

"Why, yes, of course that is true," he answered. "But first of all you have to choose your scholars, because there are scholars who believe just the opposite—many of them. One of the naïvetés to get rid of when you get into higher education is the idea that scholars agree on anything. Whether you are talking about religion or philosophy or science or poetry or art or politics or economics or anything at all, there is nothing that all scholars agree about. The first thing you have to do is to pick your scholars."

What does that have to do with happiness being a choice?

You may have come across a member of the Society of Long Faces or a member of the Fraternal Order of Gloom. Consciously or unconsciously, they have purposed to be unhappy, to greet the people and circumstances of their lives with thumbs down. They are like the old man in the Li'l Abner comic strip who, over his head, always had a black cloud raining on him. They have a list of complaints in their pockets. Just give them the chance, and you will hear every one of them read aloud. They will explain that there are objective, external causes for their dejection. The harpies of unhappiness are always pursuing them. This person mistreats them and that problem is cramping their lifestyle. Any reasonable person could see they have no choice but to be unhappy.

Not so! We have a choice, and God commands us to make the right one, to make the choice that will glorify him and benefit ourselves. Pick your scholars. You can either dwell on the unpleasant people, places, and events in your life, or you can dwell on the love of God: his forgiveness, his promises, his provisions for your life.

One day two great men, Charles Spurgeon and Theodore Keiler, having just completed a series of important meetings, took a walk through the countryside. A great weight had been lifted off their shoulders, and they played like kids out in the woods. Keiler told a story that suddenly struck Spurgeon's funny bone, and he began to laugh heartily until his whole frame shook. When Spurgeon could finally stop laughing and dry his eyes, he told Keiler, "Theodore, let us get down on our knees at once and thank God for laughter."

Prayer and laughter are not strangers. Each one of us needs to start our day with the prayer, "This is the day which the LORD hath made; we will rejoice and be glad in it" (Psalm 118:24). Determine to fulfill that, knowing that "... at thy right hand there are pleasures [joy] for evermore" (Psalm 16:11b).

DON'T WAIT FOR TOMORROW

Why aren't people happier? What can be done to rejoice in the day?

Begin by determining what you will dwell on, what you will attend to: what people, what events, what circumstances. Paul wrote, "... if there be any virtue, if there be any praise, if there be any good report, think on these things. Those things, which ye have both learned, and received, and heard, and seen in me, do: and the God of peace shall be with you" (Philippians 4:8b-9). And Jesus said, "These things have I spoken unto you, that my joy might remain in you, and that your joy might be full" (John 15:11).

The philosophy of existentialism contains a truth that the psalmist affirms in our key verse: "This is the day which the LORD hath made; we will rejoice and be glad in it." We need to focus on the present moment to the exclusion of the past or future. We are to seize the day, the moment, and rejoice and be glad in it. We do not leave our happiness in the past. We do not wait until tomorrow to be glad. We rejoice and exude gladness *today*. Right now. Pay attention to what is going on. Keep your eye on the ball of life.

It is like the art of reading aloud. You must put the emotion and the impact you want to convey right on the word you are speaking. You can't let your thoughts race three or four words ahead of what you are actually saying—or the passage does not come across to the audience with the meaning or impact it should have. Similarly, don't think about rejoicing tomorrow. Think about rejoicing today, and do it!

Unlike the atheistic existentialist who blocks out the past and the future, the Christian can perceive and enjoy events for the value they have. The Christian can look back to the crucifixion and the resurrection and be forgiven, cleansed, and renewed. Christ has disposed of the sin, the shame, the guilt, the failures. By looking back, we Christians can know and remember that we are new persons in Christ's family. This is a great cause for rejoicing and being glad.

As Christians we look ahead and boldly affirm that there is a glorious tomorrow. We eagerly anticipate the return of Christ, who will usher in a paradise free of pain and tears and death. The sovereign Lord is the Lord of tomorrow, and he works all things together for the Christian's good.

MONITOR YOUR THOUGHTS

For this reason we must monitor our thoughts, those steady streams of conversation in our heads, and pinpoint what puts a dirty film over the windows of the soul, a film that filters out the sparkle and the joy. That film may be worry, anxiety, and speculation over uncertainties, doubts, problems with ramifications, challenges, trials, uncomfortable situations, needs, wants.

Consciously endeavor to say, "The Lord is the Lord of tomorrow, and I will cast all my cares on him because he cares for me. I am going to think about the good things of God to keep the windowpanes clean that my soul might sparkle with his joy."

My friend, in Christ lies the only secret of happiness. We can reach back into the past to the cross and find in faith the answer to the problems of sin and guilt and shame and failure. We can reach forward in hope to his coming again and to his promises of a glorious future, dispelling all discouragement and despondency and hopelessness and gloom. The past and the future, faith and hope—they work together in the present for a love that bubbles with joy. The fact that God is working all things together for our good right now enables us to say each morning: "This is the day which the LORD hath made; we will rejoice and be glad in it."

As you rejoice, expect God to use your joy for his purposes. The great preacher F.B. Meyer said that he was brought to Christ by observing the exuberant joy in the face of a young man who had recently committed his life to God. The joy was contagious. Meyer said that to see it was to hunger after it and to desire it with all one's soul. So he sought it; he found it; and he, too, went on his way rejoicing.

That young man may never have known how God used that smile on his face to expand the Lord's kingdom. You see, as you mature in Christ, he steps in in unexpected ways to transform your world and your relationships.

FOR REFLECTION

Imagine yourself in prison like Paul and Silas. Would you be able to sing praises to God throughout the night?

Can you imagine anyone—friend, family member, or stranger—being drawn to God because of the joy evident on your face?

Consider James 4:8: "Draw nigh to God, and he will draw nigh to you." How can this verse help you monitor your thoughts today? What does this verse tell you about delighting in God—and delighting God?

Part Three

Transforming Your World and Your Relationships

TWELVE

How to Have Love in Your Marriage

This love of which I speak is slow to lose patience—it looks for a way of being constructive. It is not possessive; it is neither anxious to impress nor does it cherish inflated ideas of its own importance. Love has good manners and does not pursue selfish advantage. It is not touchy. It does not keep account of evil or gloat over the wickedness of other people. On the contrary, it is glad with all good men when truth prevails. Love knows no limit to its endurance, no end to its trust, no fading of its hope; it can outlast anything. It is, in fact, the one thing that still stands when all else has fallen. 1 Corinthians 13:4-8 (J.B. Phillips)

I'M OLD ENOUGH TO REMEMBER a once-popular song that went like this: "What is this thing called love? This funny thing called love?" It's a question that can be asked—and answered—on many levels. When answered in a biblical context, it's a question that can transform your world and your relationships.

Let's start with the most intimate of relationships—marriage. I am convinced that many people do not know what love really means. In a magazine I recently read about an actress who was getting married because (can you believe it?) she was *in love*. And it was really going to work this time, because she was *really* in love. The other three times she had thought she was in love, but she'd been wrong. This time she was sure....

Forgetting the actress faraway in her Hollywood world, right in my office I have counseled how many—too many—young engaged couples that have boldly proclaimed their love. But hardly two years later they are axing each other to death in a divorce court. What happened to that undying love that was going to last until the stars go out, until the mountains fade away? It must be some sort of a mystery! "Ah, sweet mystery of life; at last I've found you"—another old song. Love, true love. What is this mysterious thing called love?

TWO VIEWS OF LOVE

It seems to come, almost to descend mysteriously, upon some couples like an ethereal bird of paradise. It hovers above them and flaps its enchanting wings and causes their hearts to palpitate for a while and then, alas, sometimes all too soon, it flies away. It is a mystery. We just can't understand it. It is a strange thing, yet when you read the Bible there doesn't seem to be any sort of mysterious quality like that connected with love.

First Corinthians 13 is *the* classic chapter on love in all of literature. Is there anything mysterious about it? It deals with very down-to-earth, straightforward, plain sorts of things—not the glazed-eye view we hear about in romantic love songs. Actually, the romantic concept of love has so pervaded modern culture that I would imagine the vast majority of people in America believe that's what love is. But this romantic view of love came to the fore in literature with Johann Wolfgang von Goethe, the German poet and writer who wrote in the early nineteenth century. And this view is now so widely accepted that to challenge it seems almost heresy.

What is love? If you ask a lot of people, as I have, you will get an answer like this, "Well, love is a... it's a wonderful thing." True. But what kind of thing is it? "Well, it's... it's a wonderful feeling that you get down inside of you." Right? Wrong! Love is not a feeling. The romantic writers and the Hollywood script writers have been so successful in passing off the romantic concept of love that some people are shocked at this. "Of course that is what love is! Why, it's this wonderful feeling!" Is it? Let us consider again the inspired definition of love:

Charity [love] suffereth long, and is kind; [love] envieth not; [love] vaunteth not itself, is not puffed up, Doth not behave itself unseemly, seeketh not her own, is not easily provoked, thinketh no evil; Rejoiceth not in iniquity, but rejoiceth in the truth; Beareth all things, believeth all things, hopeth all things, endureth all things. [Love] never faileth. 1 Corinthians 13:4-8a

"Love never faileth." And yet this thing we call love has a most remarkable record of failure, has it not?

It would appear that either God doesn't have a clue as to what love is (and we might remember that God is love) or else most Americans don't have a clue as to what love is, because I would point out that there is not a "tingle" in that whole passage. There is not even a palpitation! What is there? Analyze it.

LOVING ACTIONS, LOVING ENDURANCE

There are two things. First, there are actions taken—good, kindly actions, thoughtful actions. On the other hand, there are things endured—unkind things that are borne, endured with patience and kindness.

I find it interesting that the life of Jesus Christ is divided by theologians into two parts: his active obedience and his passive obedience.

His active obedience is everything he did. And what did he

do? He reached out his hand to open the eyes of the blind; he fed the poor; he lifted up the downcast; he forgave the sinner; he comforted the mourner. As it says in Acts 10:38, he "went about doing good."

His passive obedience—from which we get the word *passion*—involves that which he endured. He endured the mockery, the laughter, the betrayal of his friends. He endured the slapping, the spitting, the crown of thorns, the scourge, the nails in the hands and feet, and his final agony on the cross.

And so you see that we have embodied in the active and passive obedience of Christ the perfect embodiment of love as it is defined in 1 Corinthians 13. The loving actions and loving endurance is ignored by the romanticist writers who vainly search for that sweet mystery of life, that bird of paradise, that Cupid's arrow that falls out so easily. Yet this is what love really is.

NOT BASED ON FEELINGS

Some time ago a woman said to me, "I don't love my husband anymore. I just don't love him. I haven't loved him for a number of years. There is no love in our home. Don't you agree that what I ought to do is get a divorce?"

Now what do you say to a person who says that? I said, "Well, that is terrible. I am sorry to hear that. Tell me about it. Did you ever love him?"

"Oh yes, when I married him I loved him. He was so kind and considerate then, but after we were married he began to drink and treat me indifferently. Then he began to treat me badly. I lost all love for him."

She continued, "But you know, once I became very sick and had an operation, and while I was in the hospital, he changed. He brought me flowers and candy, sat on the bed, held my hand, and read to me. It's the strangest thing, but I began to love him again at that time."

I said, "No kidding! That is really mysterious, isn't it?"

She said, "Yes, but it went away. After I got out of the hospital, it wasn't too long before he began drinking again. I just haven't had any love for him for years. There is just nothing else to do. Don't you agree that I ought to get a divorce if I just don't love him?"

I said, "I'll tell you what I believe the Bible would have you do. If you just *don't* love your husband, if you just don't love him at all, then the Bible would say that you ought to go home, get down on your knees, and repent of your sin."

She was shocked. You see the Bible doesn't offer us a wish that we could love our husbands or wives. It isn't a fond hope; it isn't "Good luck. Congratulations. We hope you have a happy life" (all of the time thinking, "I hope it lasts three years").

It isn't a good wish; it is a command! The Scripture says, "Husbands, love your wives" (Ephesians 5:25). "Wives, submit yourselves unto your own husbands" (Ephesians 5:22). It isn't a wish. It is a commandment from God. If you don't do it, you are sinning against God, and you need to repent of that sin.

But you say, "How can I command a feeling?" That is just the point I am trying to make! Love isn't a feeling. You cannot command a feeling. And yet God commands you to love your husband or wife. He is not talking about feelings. He is talking about these things that I have just read about. Love suffereth long; love seeketh not its own, is not easily provoked. Love is concerned for the other person, seeks the welfare of its partner. These things we can do.

AS I HAVE LOVED YOU

Jesus said, "This is my commandment, That ye love one another, as I have loved you" (John 15:12). How does God love? When the Bible says that God loves us, that doesn't mean that God just gets all gooey inside when he thinks about us. When God looks down at me, he doesn't have heart palpitations. John 3:16 says that "God so loved the world, that he gave his only begotten Son" to a world sunk deep in the quagmire of sin—in the quagmire of all sorts of lying, hating, lust-ing, stealing, cheating, pride, and vanity. God looks down at that, and he doesn't like it. God doesn't like sin, but he loves sinners. That means that he has set his heart and mind that he is going to do unto us good. It means that his love never dies; it suffers long.

Many people get married on the basis of infatuation and then wonder why their love doesn't last. *Infatuation* comes from the Latin word *infatuare*, which has two roots: *in* plus *fatuus*. *Fatuous* (though spelled differently in Latin) means the same thing as it does in English. It means "foolish." There are people who base their lives and homes upon the foolishness of infatuation and have the added foolishness of calling it love, and then wonder whatever happened.

I sometimes liken it to the fragrance of a rose. You know what a rose is, and I say that a rose is a delightful aroma, a lovely fragrance. You say, "No, that is not quite right. A rose is a flower, and it produces a fragrance and an aroma, but the fragrance isn't the flower. I'm a little bit confused." Well, a lot of people are just similarly confused about love. When we love as directed in 1 Corinthians 13, one of the by-products is a good feeling—the fragrance. But the real love, the real rose, is the actions and the patient endurance—the love that is like Christ's love.

TENDING THE DELICATE FLOWER OF LOVE

The problem with many people—including the woman who wanted to get a divorce because she no longer loved her husband—is that they once planted a rose in their garden, and they have gone out each day to smell the fragrance. But over the years they have trampled on that rose and stomped it into the mud until finally it has disappeared beneath the ground altogether. Then, one day, they wake up and say, "Ah, the fragrance is gone. What shall I do?"

Well, the rose needs to be brought up from under the mud of abuse. A rose is not a particularly mysterious thing, but it is a delicate thing. And love is a delicate thing and needs to be handled gently, or you will wonder where the fragrance went. That happens in a lot of marriages. But true love can make a marriage the closest thing to heaven on earth that we can know.

There was another popular song when I was a young man. This was, I think, the first song ever written by hippies—and there wasn't even a hippie on the horizon in those days. It was called "Nature Boy." There was this strange boy. I don't know exactly what kind of a boy he was, but I can imagine this nature boy walking around the woods with his robe and long hair and staff and declaring his message. I was touched by that message, which I've never forgotten. He said, "The greatest thing you'll ever know, is just to love and be loved in return."

Let me say that again, because if you empty that of the romantic concept of love and pour into it the biblical concept, I think he is dead right. "The greatest thing you'll ever know, is just to love and be loved in return." To love God and to be loved by him, to love others and to be loved by them, to have love in your marriages and homes and to be loved by family—that is the greatest thing you'll ever know.

Do you have that great thing in your life? Or have you trampled the rose in the mud and lost the fragrance? You can have that love in your home again. How are you going to do it? You're going to do it when you realize that infatuation is not love, that lust is not love. Though these things are natural, the love about which the Bible speaks and the love that can transform a home into paradise upon earth is an absolutely unnatural thing. It is unnatural to humankind in its fallen state. It is a supernatural thing.

LOVE—NOT IN OUR OWN STRENGTH

We humans are essentially selfish, turned inward upon ourselves; by nature we seek to fulfill our own desires and are everything this passage tells us not to be. You say, "I just can't be that other way." You are right! You may be like that for a few weeks but not for long. The only way that anyone is ever going to do this is to realize that he or she can't. We must realize that God is love and we are selfish and that our vessels must be filled with God. That is why those who try to make their homes happy and ignore God, the fountain and source of love, are chasing a rainbow they will never find. We need to be filled with God's love. This means, first of all, that we need to have come to know and experience the love of God. We need to have been justified by faith in Christ.

Psychiatrists and psychologists have discovered that a child is not, even on the most rudimentary level, able to love unless that child has been loved. It is a tragedy when some parents, feeling unloved themselves, have a child so that the child will love them. If the child is brought into the world to provide that which is lacking in the parent, the vicious circle continues. Only the love of Jesus Christ breaking in can end it.

We need to experience and to know the love of Jesus Christ, then we'll be able to love. The *King James Version* of the Bible says, "We love him, because he first loved us" (1 John 4:19). But the word *him* is in italics, which means that it is not in the Greek text. The Greek text says, "We love because he first loved us." Unless you have come to know the love of God in Jesus Christ, you will never be able to love anyone else. The only way you are going to know that is to realize how unworthy you are, what a sinner you are—as I have come to realize about myself—and to place your trust in the Cross of Christ, who for the love that he had for us, endured the shame and the agony of the cross and died in our place. If we will cease to trust in any supposed goodness in ourselves, cease to trust in any love that we have to others or to God, and put our trust in the love of God for us revealed in the cross, then we will experience the love of God and our hearts will be changed.

That is the first thing, but it is not the only thing. There are people who have accepted Christ as Savior and Lord, and yet they have not experienced the joy of love in their homes. Why? Because they have not yielded themselves completely to God. They have never truly surrendered themselves wholeheartedly to God. I am utterly convinced that the miserable marriages so rampant today, even in the church, are simply the price people pay for unyielded lives to God. Homes that are a little bit of hell on earth are the dividend the devil pays for our faithfulness to him and our infidelity to God.

MAKE LOVE YOUR AIM

The first verse of 1 Corinthians 14 begins with the phrase that many commentators believe should be the last phrase in chapter 13. It says, "Follow after charity [love]." It might be translated "Pursue after love." The verb is used to describe Paul when he was pursuing the Christians to persecute them. It is the word that he used when he said, "I press toward the mark for the prize of the high calling of God in Christ Jesus" (Philippians 3:14). It is an active and energetic seeking, searching, and reaching forward toward something. I think "Follow after love" could be translated, "Make love your aim."

Determine that you are going to pray for the love of Jesus Christ to fill your heart and overflow into your marriage. This Christ who can make all things new can give you a new beginning in your home. Determine that you are going to study to find out what love is and that you are going to pursue its application in your home. Then, by the grace of God, he who is love himself—coming to live in yielded hearts—can make any home a little bit of heaven. Yes, God can put love in your home. Will you, in your home, make love your aim?

FOR REFLECTION

In the context of your marriage, consider the two parts of love: loving actions and loving endurance. What can you do this week to pursue love in your home?

If unforgiveness is a stumbling block to your marital relationship, the next chapter will provide more insights into transforming your relationships through forgiveness.

THIRTEEN

How to Forgive Your Friends and Enemies

And forgive us our debts, as we forgive our debtors.... For if ye forgive men their trespasses, your heavenly Father will also forgive you. But if ye forgive not men their trespasses, neither will your Father forgive your trespasses.

Matthew 6:12, 14-15

AROUND THE WORLD Christians say the Lord's Prayer weekly, even daily. "And forgive us our debts, as we forgive our debtors." But do most of us have any idea of the real implications of what we say by rote?

There is no question about the meaning of this line of Jesus' prayer. He even goes on immediately after the prayer to clarify his point: "For if ye forgive men their trespasses, your heavenly Father will also forgive you. But if ye forgive not men their trespasses, neither will your Father forgive your trespasses." By the inordinate emphasis given to forgiveness in this explanation, Jesus reminds us of how important forgiveness is.

Think of it. Have you invited anger, wrath, tribulation, and condemnation upon your head? You say, "But just a minute!

Doesn't the Bible teach that we are saved and forgiven by faith and repentance, rather than by forgiving other people?"

Yes, we are saved by faith. But here Christ teaches that the same repentance and faith in Christ that, when directed to God in heaven, results in our salvation will inevitably, when directed toward other humans, result in our forgiving them their trespasses.

Christians are the society of the forgiven, and if they are, they are inevitably the society of the forgiving. Christ has made it clear that we cannot be sons and daughters of God if we will not be brothers and sisters.

WHAT IS FORGIVENESS?

What is the meaning of the verb to forgive? The Greek word means "to put away, to abandon, to forget, to cast off." The English word *forgive* comes from the Anglo-Saxon word *forth-given*, which means "that which we give forth."

But I think perhaps the meaning of forgiveness was expressed more clearly by a little boy who never knew the root words yet understood something of the real essence of it. When he was asked, "What is forgiveness?" he said, "Forgiveness is the fragrance a flower gives off when it is stepped on."

Question: What kind of flower are you—a rose or a stinkweed? What kind of fragrance or odor do you give off when you are trampled on? Do you smell like a rose or stinkweed? Forgiveness—"forth-giving"—what we give off when we are hurt or harmed.

BUT HOW CAN I FORGIVE SUCH A TRESPASS?

"It hurts! How can I forgive?"

It seems we have so much difficulty forgiving other people, and most of the time we hold our grudges for the slightest slights. Peccadilloes—no more. An unkind word or a slighting action or a bit of forgetfulness. Maybe a look, a cocking of the head, a glance—some small insult to our dignity.

Well, consider just a few scenarios I've read about in the newspapers:

He was eighty years old. In a downpour he picked up a drenched couple that needed help. He took them to his home and let them call for help on his telephone. But the couple brutally beat and robbed him. They took his car and drove away. *How can this man forgive?*

Another man: The forearms, feet, legs, and head of his twenty-nine-year-old daughter had just been found on the river bank. Two suspects had been picked up. *How can he forgive?*

A third: This father's son had just completed his bar exam and was preparing to start his career as a lawyer. The son was killed in a traffic shooting on the interstate highway. The man arrested has a record of seventeen arrests for armed robbery, cocaine possession, and other crimes, yet he was acquitted. *How can this father forgive?*

What is it that you have difficulty forgiving somebody for? A word? A look? A slight? No matter what your situation, your question "How will I be able to forgive?" can be answered by asking another question—asked by a farmer I read about some years ago.

Someone had broken into this man's home and killed ten members of his family, including his wife. He himself had been shot four times—the only one to survive. After the murderer had served his twenty-year prison term, the authorities would not let him out because he had nowhere to go. Hearing this, the farmer offered to take him into his home. He said, "Christ died for my sins and forgave me. Should I not forgive this man?"

MUST I FORGIVE?

"Well, should I forgive them even if they don't ask me for forgiveness?" For some years I thought that our forgiveness should be predicated upon someone requesting our forgiveness and repenting. Is it not true that God doesn't forgive us until we ask him for his forgiveness?

And then there is Peter's question of Jesus: "Then came Peter to him, and said, Lord, how oft shall my brother sin against me, and I forgive him? till seven times? Jesus saith unto him, I say not unto thee, Until seven times: but, Until seventy times seven" (Matthew 18:21-22). But Luke gives a slightly different turn: "And if he trespass against thee seven times in a day, and seven times in a day turn again to thee, saying, I repent: thou shalt forgive him" (Luke 17:4). In Luke, the brother came and repented.

In this and in other instances, Christ says that if a person asks for forgiveness we are to offer forgiveness.

But upon further and long reflection and consideration, I have come to believe that we are to forgive others whether or not they ask for forgiveness.

The greatest example Christ gave of forgiveness was on the cross when he said, "Father, forgive them; for they know not what they do" (Luke 23:34a). If you remember that scene, people were not imploring Christ to forgive them. No such utterance escaped from their lips. They were, indeed, mocking him. They were reviling him. They were cursing him. And yet Jesus said, "Father, forgive them, for they know not what they do."

Subsequently the thief being crucified next to Jesus said, "Jesus, Lord, remember me when thou comest into thy kingdom" (Luke 23:42). And though it is true that God forgives us when we come in faith and repentance to him, asking for it, in a deeper sense we never come to him unless he first, by his Spirit, draws us unto him.

This is so beautifully expressed in the words of an old hymn, dating from 1893 by George W. Chadwick:

> I sought the Lord, and afterward I knew
> he moved my soul to seek him, seeking me;
>
> it was not I that found, O Savior true;
> no, I was found of thee.

Yes, it is our responsibility to forgive, as Christ freely invites us to be reconciled to him.

THE FIVE "R'S"

Nothing is so Christlike as to forgive our enemies—to forgive those who have done us great evil. The problem most of us have is not forgiving our enemies. We can't even forgive our loved ones for those "horrendous things" they have done! Peccadilloes, usually, and yet hurts that call for a fragrant forgiveness.

How do we take the first difficult step? Let me give you five quick suggestions. To make it easy, I've started them all with the letter R.

Recognize. We need to recognize how many times we need to forgive people. Sometimes we don't forgive because we are not even aware of the fact that as Christians we are bound to forgive.

How can we recognize the need to forgive? A couple of clues might help. When you get ready to blow up and get angry with somebody, you probably have something you need to forgive them for. Or maybe you are not someone who explodes. You're the tortoise type; you just draw your head inside your shell and give the old silent treatment. Is that you?

Or maybe you have the desire to get even. You don't get mad; you just get even! That's written on the walls of hell. So if you find yourself blowing up or drawing in or bristling every time you see someone or mapping out your strategies for getting even, you need to recognize the times: It's time to walk the road of forgiveness.

Remember. We need to remember Christ if we are going to have any opportunity to forgive, because only Christ enables people to forgive. No other religion really enables people to forgive their enemies. We need to remember the Messiah who said, "Father forgive them, for they know not what they do."

When Harry Ironsides, one of the famous preachers in the

early decades of this century, was an old man, he remembered an incident that took place when he was a boy, seven or eight years old.

Some men from the church were meeting in his home, sitting around the table. Harry was on the other side of the living room, paying no attention to the boring subjects they were discussing, until the tones changed. The volume increased, the pitch went up, and anger filled the room.

Finally somebody slammed his fist on the table, jumped up, knocked his chair over backward, and said, "There are a lot of things I'll put up with, but I will not stand for somebody trying to put something over on me like that. I have my rights!"

At this point an old Scotsman at the table leaned forward and said, "Aye, what'd ya say? I couldna hear ya."

The man answered, "I have my rights!"

"Oh, mon, surely ya didna mean that. If ya got yer rights, yu'd go right to hell, 'cause that's wot ya deserve, and have ya fergott'n that Jesus came not to get his rights, but to take our wrongs?"

Suddenly it seemed like everything inside the angry man just collapsed. He fell back and said, "I'm sorry, brethren, I was wrong. Settle it any way you like."

He remembered Christ. And that is the key to forgiveness—to remember him, who took our wrongs and prayed for our forgiveness.

Release. We need not only recognize the situation and remember Christ, but we need to *release* the offenders from our judgment. Catherine Marshall said that the essence of forgiveness is to release a person from our judgment.

When somebody does us wrong, we're often like the servant in Jesus' parable who owed the king ten thousand talents of gold. He came and implored the king, who had mercy upon him and forgave him that enormous debt.

This servant went out and found a fellow servant who owed him a hundred pence—just a matter of pennies. The man with the upper hand took the debtor by the throat and said, "Pay me." But he could not pay and begged for mercy. No, the man who had received mercy for a huge debt would not forgive a small debt. The servant cast the man into prison until he would pay the entire amount.

How many people have you cast into your prison? How about your dungeon, your anger and wrath down deep in the subterranean cellar of your soul? How many people do you have chained to those cold damp walls? Perhaps there are even iron collars around their throats. Now and again, you open the creaking door and go down into that dank dungeon to see how you might torment them. Forgiveness is letting them go— releasing them from your judgment.

Catherine Marshall recommended that we verbally walk through this release. When I read her advice, there was some-one who had done great harm to my dignity. I was like a tightly wound spring, recognizing my need to forgive. One night lying in bed, I said the words out loud: "Lord, right now I release this person from my judgment." A sense of great peace flooded my soul, and soon I was ready for sleep. We need to release from our judgment those who have done us wrong.

When somebody has wronged you, remember Jesus' parable about the servant forgiven of a great debt of ten thousand tal-ents of gold who would not forgive a debt of a hundred pence. When you see the person who has offended you, say, "There goes a hundred-pence man." "There goes a hundred-pence woman." When you do that you will be amazed how that shrinks the offense and reminds you of the enormous debt you have been forgiven. You will take a long leap toward releasing the offense.

Resolve. We need to resolve to overcome evil with good. Again, we don't have to wait until an offender has come and asked for forgiveness, as Jesus did not. But try it: As you forgive someone, do something good instead of something evil for that person. This will do more good than you can imagine for you and for them. As hard as it might be, it will help you to forgive.

What a glorious thing it is to do good unto those who have

done evil to us. Phillips Brooks, an Episcopal bishop in the nineteenth century, gave us the wonderful Christmas carol "O Little Town of Bethlehem." He was a great hulk of a man— about six and a half feet tall. Somebody said that until you had done Phillips Brooks an injury, you never felt the full brunt of his love.

I think that is one of the most spectacular comments ever made about a mortal Christian. May God grant us the grace that it might be said about us—as we resolve to overcome evil with good.

Rejoice. Earlier in this same Matthew passage—the Sermon on the Mount—Jesus said, "Blessed are ye, when men shall revile you, and persecute you, and shall say all manner of evil against you falsely, for my sake. Rejoice, and be exceedingly glad: for great is your reward in heaven" (Matthew 5:11-12a).

Rejoice? In a previous chapter we've already talked about our joy being determined not by externals but by our relationship with Christ. It's hard to rejoice while you're harboring unforgiveness in your heart.

Jesus says we are to rejoice, being aware of the rewards of heaven. But we have more than a great reward in heaven. We also have a great witness right here. Nothing witnesses so powerfully as when a Christian forgives an enemy.

A POWERFUL WITNESS

Some years ago there was a war among the Turks—Muslim Turks and Christian Turks. One of the Christian officers was captured and made a prisoner of a Muslim official who treated the Christian with the utmost cruelty and hatred.

But then the circumstances of the war changed. That Christian prisoner was released; the torturer was captured. When he realized that he was in the hands of the same Christian whom he had abused, the Muslim's eyes filled with fear of retaliation and vengeance. But the Christian man said, "Do not be afraid. I am a Christian, and I will not return evil for evil; I forgive you for what you did to me."

The astonished Muslim said, "I will not die a Muslim, but I will die a Christian, for no other faith teaches forgiveness of injuries."

What a marvelous testimony—to do good to them who have done evil to us.

"Forgive us our debts as we forgive our debtors." Next time you pray those words consider their meaning. By harboring unforgiveness against a friend or an enemy, are you destroying your own physical life as well as your spiritual life? Are you delighting God or making him wince in pain?

FOR REFLECTION

When someone tramples on you, what fragrance do you give forth? That of a rose? Or a stinkweed?

If there is a particular person you have not forgiven, walk through the five R's with that person in mind. Recognize your unforgiving spirit. Remember that you can forgive only by the power of Christ—not of yourself. Release that person from your judgment. Speak the words aloud. Resolve to overcome evil with good. Rejoice in the Lord always—even when you are criticized by others.

FOURTEEN

How to Receive—and Give—Criticism

The Son of man is come eating and drinking; and ye say, Behold a gluttonous man, and a winebibber, a friend of publicans and sinners! Luke 7:34

S OME PEOPLE ARE VERY CREATIVE in the way they handle criticism. For example, Dwight L. Moody, the Billy Graham of a century or more ago, once mounted the pulpit to preach to a vast audience. He looked down and saw that someone had placed a one-word note on his pulpit: "Fool!" He picked it up, examined it, and replied, "I have received a lot of messages where the writer failed to sign his name, but I believe this is the first time I have seen the writer sign his name and forget the message!"

Well, we all may not be as creative as Moody, but one thing is certain, we are all going to receive some share of the criticism this world has to offer. Criticism, the "lemons of life" it has been called. Let me suggest three things you can do that might help you better handle criticism.

PREPARE TO RECEIVE CRITICISM

First, get ready to duck because the lemons are surely coming your way. There is no way you can really avoid it. One public official had these words embroidered and placed on his wall: "To avoid criticism: Do nothing, say nothing, be nothing."

That's reminiscent of the words of Joseph Addison: "There is no defense against reproach except obscurity."

I doubt that even obscurity is a sure defense against reproach, because it doesn't matter how high or how low you are in station in this world, you are going to experience some degree of criticism. If you follow the "do nothing, say nothing, be nothing" advice, you'll be called a nothing, and quite caustically.

Some people whose names are never going to be written in lights live with professional critics who criticize them day in and out.

Then if you rise just a little bit above the common herd, if you achieve just a modicum more of success than your neighbor, most surely those barbs of criticism are going to be shot your way.

As Jonathan Swift said, "Censure is the tax a man pays to the public for being eminent."

Everybody is criticized sometime or another.

Have you ever been criticized? Have you ever been criticized unjustly? We have a tendency to assume that *all* the criticism we receive is unjust, but even an objective observer would no doubt say that at least some of the criticism any of us receives is just.

Let us remember Christ who endured unjust criticism for our sake. Here was Jesus Christ, the only person who ever lived who actually did nothing for which he could be justly criticized—the Great Exemplar, the Crystal Christ, that one in whom there is nothing in which anyone could justly find fault. Yet Jesus himself, the perfect man, was called a glutton, a drunkard, a carouser, an illegitimate child, a fraud, a revolutionary, a sabbath breaker, a lunatic, an imposter, a liar, a charlatan, a blasphemer, a seditionist, a scofflaw, an extremist, a devil, a misguided martyr, a phantom, a missing corpse, a soon-to-be-forgotten misfit. What critics!

Jesus said that if they had loved him, they would love his followers, but since they have hated him, they will hate his followers (see John 15:18). If you are living a godly Christian life, the world will be sure to see that you will receive your share of criticism.

All they who live godly lives in Christ Jesus shall suffer persecution, the Bible tells us. In our country today, we can be thankful that does not include the thumbscrew or being burned at the stake, crucified, or thrown to the lions. About the most that is likely to happen to you is that people will criticize you and say bad things about you. You can be thankful that is all they are likely to do.

You might as well face it. Get ready to duck, because whoever you are, you are going to have to handle some share of the world's criticism.

MAKE LEMONADE FROM THE LEMONS

Second, I would like to suggest that when criticism comes your way, try to make lemonade out of the lemons. Benefit from your critics. Let your critics be the unpaid watchers after your soul, the beneficiaries of your career. Let them help you along the way.

George Washington Carver, from Tuskeegee Institute, urged his young students not to respond to criticism in anger but to try to see the good that might be there, regardless of the attitude or hostility of the person criticizing them.

Abraham Lincoln was quite adept at handling criticism. When told by a young woman what an abominable boor he was, how ill-mannered and illiterate he was, he took it all to heart and worked diligently to become one of the most literate men who ever lived—a man whose wit and kindliness is legend.

When Stanton called him a fool, Lincoln said, "Did Stanton

really call me a fool? Stanton is a wise man. If he said that I am a fool, then I had better look into the matter."

And Lincoln profited mightily from that criticism.

I remember clearly when the Lord called me into the ministry. Before I had finished college or gone to seminary, I was preaching temporarily in a little stone church in Clearwater, Florida. I found that the gospel seemed to be pretty alien in that church, and I can't say that it was wholly appreciated by all. In fact, I remember one rather stuffy old elder—something of a curmudgeon—who was very upset by the preaching of the gospel. He stopped me one night on a dirt road near the church in front of his house and told me that he just didn't appreciate all this preaching about salvation. He didn't think he needed that.

I tried to defend my preaching. Finally, he let go with a barb that I will probably remember, I hope without malice, for the rest of my life. He said, "Well, we prefer in the Presbyterian church that our ministers be educated men."

He turned on his heel and walked away. Well, that old fellow is long gone to his reward, and he doesn't know the impact that criticism had on my life.

I tried to take that lemon and make some lemonade. And I made a vow: I said to the Lord, "Never again will anyone be able to reject your gospel, O Christ, because I have not had adequate education to be prepared to proclaim it." Now, many years and half an alphabet of degrees later, I'm just waiting for another old elder to come up and say something like that again!

One can even make lemonade from criticism given by family members. I pity the preacher who doesn't have a wife who can be a loving and gentle critic. My own wife, Anne, has been very helpful to me over the years in helping me to improve my preaching. One minister said he wanted his wife to always criticize his sermons—but never until Monday morning—after a good breakfast.

An early edition of *The Sunday School Times* made the following suggestion: "Commit the matter instantly to God, asking him to remove all resentment or counter-criticism on our part, and to teach us any needed lesson." Some people invariably respond to criticism with counter-criticism, losing all possible advantage from it. They've never learned how to make lemonade from lemons.

THROW AWAY THE RIND

In addition to preparing yourself to receive criticism, and making lemonade out of the lemons thrown your way, let me suggest that you throw away the rind. Most people, however, throw away the lemonade and chew on the rind until they become bitter. They never profit from criticism. It always rankles their spirit and makes them miserable and the worst kind of people.

We saw that Lincoln was able to take criticism and use it to make himself a better person. It is also true that he knew how to get rid of it when that was the way it ought to be handled. He once said:

> If I tried to read, much less answer all the criticisms made of me, and all the attacks leveled against me, this office would have to be closed to all other business. I do the best I know how, the very best I can. And I mean to keep on doing this, down to the very end. If the end brings me out all wrong, ten angels swearing I had been right would make no difference. If the end brings me out all right, then what is said against me now will not amount to anything.[1]

How true that is. Lincoln was criticized. He was excoriated in the press constantly, as few men have been, and yet how many people can remember what the critics said of him? They even wrote this in a paper about President Lincoln: "Why are these people going to Africa looking for 'the missing link'? He's right there in Springfield."

But ultimately, Lincoln felt, as one minister said, "God is my public opinion."

The Scripture advises us: "Forgetting those things which are behind, and reaching forth unto those things which are before, I press toward the mark for the prize of the high calling of God in Christ Jesus" (Philippians 3:13b-14).

Marine Lieutenant Clebe McClary had an apt license plate on his car in this regard: FIDO, standing for "Forget It, Drive On."

Forget the criticism. Forget all they have said and go on. Ultimately, God is the only one we finally have to please. If criticism would really kill you, stop and think: The skunk would have been extinct a long time ago!

Ultimately, it is not the critic who counts. No statue has ever been erected to critics. Statues are erected to men and women who have actually been in the arena, whose faces have been marred by dust and sweat and blood, who strove valiantly, who erred and came up short again and again, yet rose and continued to fight.

I hope those three suggestions will be helpful to you in receiving criticism. Be prepared for it; make lemonade out of it; and throw away the rind.

BE CAREFUL HOW YOU THROW LEMONS

Finally, let me suggest that you be careful how you give criticism, because it can devastate friends and family. It can make enemies or bring people to despair—even suicide. Your words can be mighty swords. The lives of young people who live in an atmosphere of criticism can be ruined. Some never learn to live above the negative messages they've grown up with.

If you are giving criticism, consider the framework you give it in. Keep yourself and the person you're criticizing in the proper perspective.

Dr. Erwin W. Lutzer tells about a letter written by a college student to her parents at home. Imagine receiving this shocking news:

Dear Mom and Dad:

Just thought I'd drop you a note to clue you in on my plans. I've fallen in love with a guy called Jim. He quit high school after grade eleven to get married. About a year ago he got a divorce.

We've been going steady for two months and plan to get married in the fall. Until then, I've decided to move into his apartment (I think I might be pregnant).

At any rate, I dropped out of school last week, although I'd like to finish college sometime in the future.

Mom and Dad, I just wanted to tell you that everything I've written so far in this letter is false. NONE of it is true.

But, Mom and Dad, it is true that I got a C- in French and flunked my math. It IS true that I'm going to need some more money for my tuition payments.[2]

What do you think? Do you think she got the money? I would say, gladly, she got it!

That reminded me of a church board meeting about twenty-six years ago. Just before adjourning, I said, "Gentlemen, I have a matter of considerable seriousness I feel constrained to bring up. I've been here now about seven years and I thank the Lord for the opportunities I have had. But I feel that the Lord is calling me to finish my education. I want to go on for another master's degree and a Ph.D."

Silence—which I didn't understand. To fill the silence I kept talking, "And so, I would like to have you give me a few more weeks off in the summer so I can continue my education."

"Ohhh! In the summer! Well, sure. Yes, we'd be happy to."

Afterward I meditated upon their reaction and suddenly it dawned on me. They all thought I was quitting, which wasn't my intention at all!

This illustration simply shows how it's so important to see a situation in a proper framework. What are you saying? How is it going to be received? If the criticism really is important, how can you say it in such a way as to minimize misunderstanding?

The Bible also says that there are times when we need to bring faults to someone's attention. "Brethren, if a man be overtaken in a fault, ye which are spiritual [that is going to eliminate a great many people and make the rest of us consider our own hearts], restore such a one in the spirit of meekness; considering thyself, lest thou also be tempted" (Galatians 6:1).

But note that it says this is to be done in a spirit of meekness. That's not what I see in people I'd call "carping critics"—perpetually criticizing anything and anybody. The Bible also says, "Judge not, that ye be not judged" (Matthew 7:1), meaning of course, that we should not be continually judging people, that this not be the habit of our lives.

So much criticism is destructive, not constructive. When we criticize, let us criticize behavior and not the person; praise the person even while criticizing the behavior.

Zig Ziglar likes to tell of a day in his childhood when his mother sent him out to hoe beans in the garden. Those three long rows of beans looked about three and a half miles long to an eight-year-old! But he hoed diligently and finally called his mother to come out for the inspection. She looked the job over and did what she always did when she was not pleased: She put her hands behind her back, lowered her head, cocked it over to the side, and said, "Well, son, for most boys this would be perfectly all right. But you're not most boys, you're my son, and my son can do better than this."

Note that she criticized the behavior, but she commended the young man as a very special and outstanding young man. That was one wise mother from whom we can learn a lesson applicable to all our relationships.

THE FINAL CRITIC

Of course, ultimately it is God who will be our final critic, and there is no escaping his judgment and his criticism, which is ultimately fair. The problem is that against the standard of perfection he has given, we have all fallen short. Again I refer to

The Sunday School Times quoted earlier, talking about us and our earthly critics: "Let us always remember that we ourselves are great sinners, and the one who has criticized us does not really know the worst about us."

Yet our final critic does know the worst about us and in his love, he came into the world to take upon himself that criticism or judgment that belongs to us and to endure in our stead the penalty we ought to pay.

Christ was scourged mercilessly until his entire body had been turned into one gaping wound by a Roman scourge (beaten with a three-pronged cowhide whip with pieces of sharp metal at the end that ripped open wounds). The Romans had a practice when the prisoner fainted—as he usually did—of bringing him back to consciousness by dumping a bucket of water over him. It was mixed with a caustic solution that penetrated every wound and brought him back to consciousness in screaming agony.

When I read this I saw that God had poured upon Christ all of the caustic criticism that really should come justly upon us for our true sins. He took the penalty for the worst of our sins—for those sins nobody has found out about. He endured it all in our place that we might escape the final judgment of God and be received into the very paradise of God. Christ endured it all—our criticisms, our hurts, our griefs so that we could delight in his presence forever.

FOR REFLECTION

What can you do now to prepare yourself so you can benefit from—rather than be dragged down by—any future criticism?

Are you a chronic critic, especially of family members or church members? Lay this question before God in prayer and ask him to show you where you stand. In the next twenty-four hours listen to yourself in your conversations with others. Do you praise more than criticize?

FIFTEEN

How to Deal with Grief

And the king was much moved, and went up to the chamber over the gate, and wept: and as he went, thus he said, O my son Absalom, my son, my son Absalom! Would God I had died for thee, O Absalom, my son, my son!

2 Samuel 18:33

GRIEF! HOW BROAD, how wide, is the chasm left in our hearts by the blow that severs us from that one who means more than life itself to us. But we also experience grief at lesser losses—loss of mobility if we are struck by illness, loss of a job, a home, or a pet.

How do we handle grief when it strikes us personally? What can we say when it strikes others? How can the grace and love of God somehow help us transform our pain, even despair, at such a time of bereavement?

Let me begin by saying that the effects of grief are far greater than many people realized for centuries. The results of the "grief syndrome" are more complex, more long lasting, and more devastating than people ever dreamt until about fifty years ago, when some rather amazing discoveries were made about grief.

It took a terrible tragedy to provide the laboratory where

those discoveries were made—discoveries made as a result of the famous Coconut Grove fire in Boston. Five hundred people were trapped in a flaming inferno. Many were killed, and many of those not killed were hospitalized for serious wounds and burns.

There at the Massachusetts General Hospital they discovered something they could not explain: Some of the fire victims were doing quite well. Others with similar types of injuries—no more severe or perhaps even less severe—were not healing well at all. In fact, frequently the skin grafts were rejected and progress was agonizingly slow.

A contemporary newspaper article reported that a doctor on the staff at Massachusetts General, Dr. Erich Lindemann, probed deeper into these cases and noticed a correlation. Many of these patients had been burned and also had lost loved ones in the fire. Those who could face up to and express their grief over the loss of a loved one were generally "on the mend" physically. But in the case of those who had lost loved ones but had not been able to deal adequately with the grief of their loss, their skin grafts wouldn't take. Their wounds wouldn't heal.

LET YOURSELF MOURN

The doctor discovered something that repeated investigations since then have shown to be true. Unless grief is properly dealt with, unless it is faced squarely and the loss is acknowledged and mourned, in some way, at some time, the grief will come out—either in the healthy release of tears or in some other psychological or physical manifestation.

The psychological effects of unresolved grief include:

- terrible dejection;
- a loss of interest in the real world;
- a loss of capacity to love;
- curtailment of all meaningful activity;
- feelings of self-reproach, which result in feelings of being punished or fear and expectation of punishment.

In addition, there may be feelings of hostility, guilt, fear, bewilderment, and loneliness. How great is the pain of grief!

Physical manifestations of grief include: tightness of the throat, choking, shortness of breath, continual sighing, muscular weakness, painful inner tension. Such physical manifestations often appear every time the painful loss of the loved one returns to the grieving person, whether the thought is stimulated by meeting a sympathetic friend or by seeing some object the loved one left behind.

Delayed grief reactions can include common physical ailments such as rheumatoid arthritis, asthma, and colitis. A disruption of the whole bodily chemistry can be caused by repressed grief. Indeed, grief will come out—sometime, somewhere, some way.

When it is not properly faced and acknowledged, grief sometimes expresses itself in:

- bursts of energy and enthusiasm about the strangest kinds of activities;
- withdrawal and social isolation—even from family members and friends;
- volatility and irritability about the least little thing;
- sometimes terrific hostility and blame shifting—pointing the finger at doctors or at medics or at others who had not done something that they felt should have been done—hostility that sometimes resulted in complete schizophrenia;
- a punishing of the self based on feelings of guilt for not having saved the loved one or for not having dealt well with the loved one before death (self-punishment could take the form of extreme generosity);
- extreme and sometimes long-lasting depression.

Reading this information you may realize that you have experienced one or more of these same symptoms as a result of your "holding in" the painful emotion of grief and not facing the reality of a loss in your life.

Your body is telling you the truth. Listen to what it says and begin to walk into—and soon past—the pain of your grief.

REMEMBER—JESUS WEPT

Sometimes people do not properly grieve because they have been taught that it is not the thing to do. They have been told that it is not proper for a Christian to grieve or mourn. After all, we have an eternal hope. We know that our loved one is far better off than ever before—that our loved one is now walking the golden streets of paradise. Being assured of this, Christians don't need to weep.

On the other side of that balance I would set these two words that outweigh all other arguments: "Jesus wept" (John 11:35). Jesus, who was the Son of Man, wept as he stood before the tomb of his friend Lazarus. In that weeping he sanctified our tears and told us that there is nothing wrong with weeping. Yes, Christians not only can but should weep at the loss of a loved one. We do a disservice to a mourner if we say, "Keep a stiff upper lip. Buck up, old man."

When my wife had cancer, a foolish young clergyman came to the hospital. My face smeared with tears, I had just left the room where my wife was in agony, and this man said to me, "Keep a stiff upper lip." I have never been so tempted to stiffen anybody's upper lip in my whole life! I thought, "You jerk." I expressed that in theological terms, of course: "O foolish man that thou art, where did you get your theological education, and why don't you go back and finish it?"

We might at least take a look at a page of the Book of Job. You will recall his comforters—his three friends who came by. When they saw Job sitting on a dung heap, agonizing, his body covered with boils, they realized the extent of his loss. They sat down next to him and said nothing for seven days. Then they made a mistake: They opened their mouths! If they had just gotten up and gone home, they would have gone down as some of the world's great comforters.

When we tell grieving people to "buck up," we have it all backward. The Bible says, "Rejoice with them that do rejoice, and weep with them that weep" (Romans 12:15). But we usually try to rejoice in the presence of those who are weeping, saying, "It could get worse, you know." And then we find someone who is rejoicing about some good fortune, and we get envious and we weep over their good fortune.

The two greatest examples of grieving in the Old Testament are those of David and Jacob. Each of them was grieving over a son: Jacob, over his son Joseph (who was not dead though Jacob thought he was), and David, who grieved and piteously lamented over the loss of his son Absalom.

Now note something about those two drastically different cases: Lamenting Jacob refused to be comforted for the loss of Joseph—a faithful, loving, and godly young man who would show what he was made of when in Egypt he withstood the temptations of both defeat and success.

Contrast Joseph with David's son Absalom, a vain, traitorous, and rebellious young man. He led a revolt to throw his father off the throne and usurp the kingdom of Israel.

As unworthy as Absalom was, David lamented over him. "O my son Absalom, my son, my son Absalom! Would God I had died for thee, O Absalom, my son, my son!" (2 Samuel 18:33b).

Each of these sons is a type in the Old Testament. Joseph, the righteous, is a type of Christ: though cast down into a dungeon, he was raised up by God and set upon a throne. He withstood the temptations of Egypt.

Absalom, on the other hand, is a type of traitor. Being ungrateful to God, he attempted to rise up in rebellion and throw the king off the throne and usurp that place. In the New Testament these two types are superimposed. The type of Joseph is Christ; there he hangs upon a cross. The type of Absalom is sinful humanity and its sin is placed on Christ, the sinless Lamb of God becoming the sinful one. God pours out his wrath upon his own beloved Son to take away our guilt and sin that we might be forgiven.

Wonder of wonders! Though we have rebelled against the high King of heaven, though we have broken his laws and trampled his commandments beneath our feet, though we have often ignored him, though we have taken his name in vain, yet our Father looks down upon you and me, his "Absaloms," and that Greater-than-David says of us, "O my son, my son. O Absalom, my son, my son." Though David could not die for his son, our Greater-than-David did die for us that we might not eternally perish as Absalom did.

God himself grieves over the wayward ones who do not turn to him.

PREVENTING AN OVERWHELMING GRIEF

Virtually everyone will eventually face the grief that comes with the loss of a loved one—a spouse, parent, child, dear friend. The pain of the loss can be exacerbated by several issues. Let's look at how we can live now to prevent unnecessary pain.

Show love now. As studies have shown, guilt can intensify one's grief. That means as a "preventative" measure, we can avoid potentially devastating grief—exacerbated by guilt—by expressing our love now. Daily. If you were to give a eulogy for your wife or husband, what would you say? Say it now while he or she can still hear it.

If you would reproach yourself for what you have not done for someone you love, what would that reproach be for? Mend your ways now, while that person still can appreciate your kindness. If you would confess your remorse and regret over something you have said or done, don't wait until your tears fall on cold, unfeeling, unhearing flesh.

Witness now. The deepest grief comes to Christians when they lose loved ones who have not come to the Savior. So I would say to you: Witness to them now—now while the day of grace is still upon us, while the sun of God's forgiveness still shines in the heaven. Tell them of the love of Christ. Urge them, implore them, beseech them to come to the Savior.

Sad to say, many Christians, because of fear or sloth or carnality or just preoccupation with the things of this world, have never taken the time or made the effort to learn how to witness effectively for Christ. They have not made the effort to find out how to be an effective witness.

If this description fits you, your conscience will reproach you when your loved ones go—you dare not think where—having never surrendered to Christ.

Witness now. If you don't know how, learn. The day will surely come when your loved ones will not be able to hear.

Perhaps you have children who don't know Christ and don't walk with the Lord. The days are fleeting; the years are passing rapidly. Soon you will be gone, and then who shall care for their souls? Witness to them now. If you truly love them, pray for them. Beseech the throne of heaven for them, and beseech them to come to Christ. As the apostle Paul addressed the Romans, "I beseech you, by the mercies of God..." (Romans 12:1), so we ought to speak to those we love.

Accept Christ now. Finally, let me say if you would avoid eternal grief—that everlasting weeping and wailing and gnashing of teeth that comes to all of those who fail to avail themselves of the opportunity of a free salvation—accept Christ.

Even now he stands before you, his arms extended, and says, "Come unto me, all ye that labour and are heavy laden, and I will give you rest" (Matthew 11:28). He wants to give you salvation. He wants to carry your grief. Let go of your pride and place your life in his everlasting arms: "Surely he hath borne our griefs, and carried our sorrows" (Isaiah 53:4a).

Our Lord wants to carry your sorrows. He wants to meet your every need.

FOR REFLECTION

What losses have you faced in the last year? How can you give yourself permission to mourn and walk through your grief and sorrow?

What can you do to prevent an unnecessarily overwhelming future grief?

SIXTEEN

How Christ Can Meet Your Every Need

Jesus said unto them, Verily, verily, I say unto you, Before Abraham was, I am. John 8:58

MADAME TOUSSAUD'S world-famous wax museum of London did an extensive study in 1975 to determine who was the most loved person in human history. They queried thousands and thousands of people to make their determination. The answer: Jesus. Why?

Probably Henry Ford knew why. He said that the most successful person would be the one who would fill the greatest need best. Ford fulfilled the great need for transportation, but that is not humankind's greatest need. Jesus Christ remains the greatest and most loved person who ever lived because he made the greatest sacrifice to fill the greatest need for the greatest number of people—the whole human race.

Humanity's greatest need is life. Without life everything else fails. Christ came that we might have it abundantly. Christ came that we might delight God and live in the center of his will. Christ came that we might see God.

TO SEE GOD IS THE SOURCE OF SPIRITUAL LIFE AND RENEWAL

To see God has been the heart cry of millions down through the centuries. "Oh that I knew where I might find him!" (Job 23:3), cried Job in the oldest book in the Bible. "Lord, shew us the Father, and it sufficeth us" (John 14:8), said the disciples. And yet God dwells in light inaccessible. He is the invisible One, the One upon whose face no one could look and live (see Exodus 33:20).

Yet Moses in a way found him—in a bush on the side of a mountain. There, as he was tending his father-in-law's sheep, he came to the backside of the desert and to Mount Horeb, the mount of God, where later the Ten Commandments would be given. There on the side of the mountain, he saw a strange sight, a bush that burned, and yet it was not consumed! Moses said, "I will now turn aside, and see this great sight, why the bush is not burnt" (Exodus 3:3).

And so, with his staff in hand, he began to climb the mountain toward this unusual sight that drew him upward. As he drew closer, a voice spoke from out of the bush saying, "Draw not nigh hither: put off thy shoes from off thy feet, for the place whereon thou standest is holy ground" (Exodus 3:5). There Moses received his commission to return to Egypt, where Pharaoh had sought his life, and deliver the children of Israel from their bondage.

Then Moses asked a question that would elicit one of the greatest revelations that humanity has ever known about God. He said,

> Behold, when I come unto the children of Israel, and shall say unto them, The God of your fathers hath sent me unto you; and they shall say to me, What is his name? what shall I say unto them? And God said unto Moses, I AM THAT I AM: and he said, Thus shalt thou say unto the children of Israel, I AM hath sent me unto you.... this is my name for ever, and this is my memorial unto all generations. (Exodus 3:13-15)

Here we have the great revelation of the name of God. In Hebrew, the relative pronoun that separates the two names can be translated in a variety of ways. It means, "I am that I am" or "I am who I am" or "I am because I am" or "I am what I am." Here is the great incomprehensible God revealing himself to Moses.

To see God—to meet God, to experience God—is the source of spiritual life, and for those who have already met him, it is the source of continued spiritual renewal.

GOD CAN BE SEEN ONLY IN THE FACE OF JESUS CHRIST

To us God has revealed not merely his name but also the express image of his person—in his Son Jesus Christ. In their comment, "Shew us the Father, and it sufficeth us" (John 14:8), the disciples were saying that seeing God would meet the deepest needs of their hearts. And what did Jesus reply? "He that hath seen me hath seen the Father" (John 14:9).

That One who had dwelt forever in light inaccessible revealed himself in the darkness of night in a stable. He revealed his brilliant light even more clearly in that midnight at noon over Golgotha, as God gave his life for the sin of the world.

People were always filled with wonder and awe at Jesus and his astonishing sayings. For example, we read of their reaction when Jesus rebuked the wind and calmed the sea: "What manner of man is this, that even the winds and sea obey him?" (Matthew 8:27).

But in John 8 we read one of Jesus' most astonishing statements. He is engaged in a controversy with the Jews, and he is telling them that they are of their father, the devil. They refuse to hear his word; they cannot hear it because they are dead in their sins. Then Jesus said, "If a man keep my saying, he shall never see death" (v. 51).

This was more than the Jews could take! They responded by saying, "Abraham is dead, and the prophets; and thou sayest, If a man keep my saying, he shall never taste of death. Art thou greater than our father Abraham, which is dead? and the prophets are dead: whom makest thou thyself?" (vv. 52b-53).

Jesus answered, "Your father Abraham rejoiced to see my day: and he saw it, and was glad." Then said the Jews unto him, "Thou art not yet fifty years old, and hast thou seen Abraham?" Jesus said unto them, "Verily, verily, I say unto you, Before Abraham was, I am" (vv. 56-58).

Many moderns reading that passage in John 8 do not grasp its full impact. But the Jews knew exactly what Jesus meant, and they took up stones to stone him for blasphemy, because he, being a man, made himself to be God.

"Before Abraham was, I am." Something about the grammar of that verse might grab your attention. Even if he had been talking about the fact that he had previously lived on this earth, you would think he would have said, "Before Abraham was, I was." Would that not be correct? To someone younger than I, I might say, "Before you were, I was." But Jesus said, "Before Abraham was, I am." Or, "Before Abraham came to be, I have always existed."

Repeatedly Jesus took this title of the great "I AM" upon his own lips. He said, "... for if ye believe not that I am *he*, ye shall die in your sins" (John 8:24). Except he didn't say that. In the *King James* Bible the word he in this verse is in italics. That means it is not in the Greek text. Jesus actually said, "Except ye believe that I am, ye shall die in your sins."

Again, this is rather strange. Jesus is standing there in person talking to the Jews. They can hear his voice; they can see him, touch him. Obviously, he is. He is right there. Wouldn't it be strange if I said, "Except that you believe that I am, you shall die in your sins." Of course, I am. Come to my church any Sunday, and you can see that I am. But again, they knew what he meant: Except you believe that I am the great I AM, you shall die in your sins.

We read in John 18 that when the temple police came to capture Jesus in the Garden of Gethsemane the night before his crucifixion, Jesus stepped forward and said, "Whom seek ye?"

They said, "Jesus of Nazareth."

And Jesus said, "I am [he]." And the soldiers "went backward, and fell to the ground" (v. 6). Jesus was showing that he was not being overwhelmed by military power and might and that he was more than capable of destroying all of these with a word. But he allowed himself to be taken. As he said, "No man taketh it [my life] from me, but I lay it down of myself. I have power to lay it down, and I have power to take it again" (John 10:18). And here he is laying it down for them.

In Mark 14:61-64, we read that when he stood before the Sanhedrin and was questioned, he was asked specifically, "Art thou the Christ, the Son of the Blessed? And Jesus said, I am."

Again they were filled with indignation: Blasphemy! "What need we any further witnesses? Ye have heard the blasphemy."

Jesus made it very plain that the great I AM who spoke to Moses on the Mount of God was the great I AM who was speaking to them and soon would be hung on an even holier mount—the Mount of Calvary.

Spiritual life and renewal comes from seeing God. And we can see God only in the face of Jesus Christ—the express image of the Father.

CHRIST CAN BE SEEN ONLY THROUGH THE EYES OF NEED

We can see Christ only through the eyes of need. We do not find him through intellectual pursuits, through philosophic contemplation, or through linguistic analysis. But through the prism of our tears we see Christ in all of his glory. As we look at him through the prism of our tears, the pure white light of Christ breaks out into all of the various colors of the rainbow, each tint meeting some specific need of our hearts.

Notice that "I AM" is really a sentence without a predicate. I am... what? "I am that I am" is simply a closed loop that could go on and on: I am that I am that I am that I am. Actually, as Roy Hession says in *We Would See Jesus*:

The name "Jehovah" is really like a blank check. Your faith can fill in what He is to be to you—just what you need, as each need arises. It is not you, moreover, who are beseeching Him for this privilege, but He who is pressing it upon you. He is asking you to ask. "Hitherto have ye asked nothing in My name: ask, and ye shall receive, that your joy may be full" (John 16:24). Just as water is ever seeking the lowest depths... Where there is need, there is God.

Where there is sorrow, misery, unhappiness, suffering, confusion, folly, oppression, there is the I AM yearning to turn man's sorrow into bliss whenever man will let Him. It is not, therefore, the hungry seeking for bread, but the Bread seeking the hungry; not the sad seeking for joy, but rather Joy seeking the sad; not emptiness seeking fulness, but rather Fulness seeking emptiness. And it is not merely that He supplies our need, but He becomes Himself the fulfilment of our need. He is ever "I am that which My people need."[1]

Dear friend, if you get a hold on that, it will change your life.

I keenly remember the day when I made that discovery—when I for the first time saw Christ through the prism of my own need, my own tears. In thinking about that, I could not help but remember another time when I saw something clearly for the first time through a different kind of prism. It was the first time I had ever gone scuba diving, a fairly new sport at the time.

There was little if any training back then. No buddy system. We went out fifteen miles off the Miami coast. They put the equipment on me, and I just jumped off the ship.

The water was crystal clear, which you couldn't tell from the ship because the wind caused quite a chop on the surface. I suddenly realized for the first time in my life that a boat floated on water—sixty feet of water. The "ocean"—the horizon—disappeared. Beneath me was a vast reef of rock. I found myself hovering six stories above "the ground" and feeling like I was falling onto the rocks below.

I tried to grab the surface of the water with my arms—no rationality involved in this at all; it was all purely instinct. Of course, the "water" had "disappeared" because of the face mask; I felt as if I were parachuting from an airplane. What an incredible revelation of something totally unseen, something that could not be seen from the deck of the ship.

So that's how I felt when I finished reading *The Greatest Story Ever Told.* In the same fateful week that I had heard the Barnhouse radio message which changed the direction of my life, I had bought Fulton Oursler's book because I wanted to learn more about this Jesus. For the first time, I looked up through the prism of the tears in my eyes, through the realization of my need, of my uncleanness, of my sin, of my iniquity, and I saw this one hanging upon the Cross of Calvary. And suddenly I knew. I knew, right then the meaning and purpose of life—to know the one true God and the Savior he sent to free me from my sins! I saw my Savior bleeding for me, and he became all that I needed:

- Unclean? He cleansed me with his precious blood.
- Without hope? He gave me his everlasting hope.
- Unrighteous? He became my righteousness.

HOW JESUS MEETS OUR NEEDS

A series of seven texts in the Old Testament are called the "Jehovah texts," where Jehovah becomes something.

The first one I discovered was *Jehovah-tsidkenu,* which means "The Lord Is Our Righteousness." In numerous Old Testament texts repeated in the New Testament, Jesus' name replaces the word *Jehovah.* He is Jehovah Jesus. And Jehovah is our righteousness.

I have asked thousands of people what righteousness their hopes of everlasting bliss are based upon. What is it they will claim and show unto God as their hope of admission to heaven? So often the answer given is simple introspection. They begin to look in at themselves.

Someone has said that we all began this life as ophthalmologists—"I" specialists. That was my answer, and it is everybody else's answer until we see Jesus through the prism of our own need and sin. "*I've* lived a good life." "*I've* kept the Ten Commandments." "*I've* followed the Golden Rule." "*I've* done the best I can." I, I, I, I, I, I.

How vain and foolish is such thinking, because all of our righteousness is but as filthy rags in the eyes of God. God demands from us a perfect righteousness without a stain or blemish. Where is your righteousness? Let me tell you about mine: *Jehovah-tsidkenu*. Jehovah Jesus is my perfect righteousness, and he clothes me with it like a white robe that I may stand faultless before his throne.

Is Jehovah Jesus your righteousness? He wants to meet that need of yours, but he does so only as you see him through the eyes of need, through the prism of tears.

The other Jehovah texts are

- *Jehovah-shalom*, "The Lord Is Your Peace,"
- *Jehovah-ra-ah*, "The Lord Is Your Shepherd,"
- *Jehovah-shammah*, "The Lord Is the One Who Is There" (wherever you are, whatever you need, he is there),
- *Jehovah-rapha*, "The Lord Is the One Who Heals,"
- *Jehovah-jireh*, "The Lord Is the One Who Provides" (whatever your need may be, Jehovah himself will become your provision),
- *Jehovah-nissi*, "The Lord Is Your Banner."

Do you want to live in the center of God's will? Can you—through the eyes of your human weakness—see Jesus as the answer to your every need? He is, says a song, "my everything."

Do you need love? He has loved us with an everlasting love.

Do you need security? It is Christ who keeps us. No one can take us out of his hands. No evil can befall us except that which he allows, and that he can work to our good. In Christ we have the only security we can have in this difficult world.

Do you need recognition? He knows his own and calls each one by name.

Do you need excitement? The mercy and grace of Jesus Christ are new each morning and fresh each day. Christ leads us on a new adventure every day. We know not whither he goes, but we know it will be a new and daring adventure with him.

Do you need self-esteem? In Christ we are children of the King of Kings. Royal blood flows in our veins. As heirs of God, our lives have a new and eternal meaning.

Jesus Christ is your everything, if you allow him to be the great I AM who will transform your world as you turn to him at every step of the way. Jesus Christ is your everything, if you open your eyes and behold him through your prism of need. Jesus Christ is your everything, if you walk in the center of his will where he will delight in you, his dear child, now and forevermore.

FOR REFLECTION

Note these words of Scripture that show how God delights in his children who walk in his will:

The LORD taketh pleasure in them that fear him, in those that hope in his mercy. (Psalm 147:11)

The steps of a good man are ordered by the LORD: and he [the Lord] delighteth in his way. (Psalm 37:23)

How can these verses help you as you look to God, the great I AM, to supply your every need and as you look to him to transform your world? Trust in him alone and in his provision for your life.

NOTES

SIX
How to Study the Bible

1. Dr. Wilbur Smith, *Profitable Bible Study* (Natick, MA: W.A. Wilde Company, 1963), 84.
2. Smith, *Profitable Bible Study,* 85.
3. Smith, *Profitable Bible Study,* 44.

SEVEN
How to Know You Have Been Born Again

1. Charles H. Spurgeon, *Autobiography of Spurgeon,* Vol. 1, 97-115, 157, and 166.

ELEVEN
How to Rejoice in Any Circumstance

1. Walter B. Knight, *Knight's Master Book of New Illustrations* (Grand Rapids: William B. Eerdman's Publishing Company, 1956), 343.

FOURTEEN
How to Receive—and Give—Criticism

1. *Encyclopedia of 7,700 Illustrations,* edited by Dr. Paul Lee Jan (Rockville, MD: Assurance Publisher, 1979), 294.
2. Dr. Erwin W. Lutzer, *Failure: Back Door to Success* (Chicago, IL: Moody Press, 1975), 19.

SIXTEEN
How Christ Can Meet Your Every Need

1. Roy Hession, *We Would See Jesus* (Fort Washington, PA: Christian Literature Crusade, 1958), 26-27.

Another Book of Interest
by D. James Kennedy

Turn It to Gold
D. James Kennedy

Whatever your disappointment, trouble, inconvenience, or grief, God promises to turn it to gold. If you trust him, God will make certain that every event that takes place in your life will pay interest to the eternal well-being of your soul.

In *Turn It to Gold*, Dr. Kennedy tackles the difficult subject of suffering in order to help you come to terms with trials and hardships in your own life. This book shows you how to turn adversity to your advantage. Your eyes will be opened to the supernatural power at work in your life that can transform every heartache to nothing short of lasting joy. *$8.99*